Media Bias in Presidential Election Coverage, 1948–2008

LEXINGTON STUDIES IN POLITICAL COMMUNICATION
Series Editor: Robert E. Denton, Jr.,
Virginia Polytechnic Institute and State University

This series encourages focused work examining the role and function of communication in the realm of politics including campaigns and elections, media, and political institutions.

RECENT TITLES IN THE SERIES:

Media Bias in Presidential Election Coverage, 1948–2008

Evaluation via Formal Measurement

Dave D'Alessio

LEXINGTON BOOKS
Lanham • Boulder • New York • Toronto • Plymouth, UK

Published by Lexington Books
A wholly owned subsidary of The Rowman & Littlefield Publishing Group, Inc.
4501 Forbes Boulevard, Suite 200, Lanham, Maryland 20706
www.rowman.com

10 Thornbury Road, Plymouth PL6 7PP, United Kingdom

British Library Cataloguing in Publication Information Available

Library of Congress Cataloging-in-Publication Data

The hardback edition was previously cataloged by the Library of Congress as follows:

D'Alessio, Dave 1956–
  Media bias in presidential election coverage, 1948–2008 : evaluation via formal
measurement / Dave D'Alessio.
    p. cm.
  Includes bibliographic references and index.
  1. Presidents—United States—Election—History. 2. Presidential candidates—Press
coverage—United States—History. 3. Political campaigns—Press coverage—United
States—History. 4. Press and politics—United States—History. 5. Journalism—
Objectivity—United States—History. 6. Mass media—Objectivity—United States—
History. I. Title
  JK524.D36 2012
  324.973'092—dc23   2012000539

ISBN 978-0-7391-6474-7 (cloth : alk. paper)
ISBN 978-0-7391-6475-4 (pbk. : alk. paper)
ISBN 978-0-7391-6476-1 (electronic)

Printed in the United States of America

Contents

List of Figures and Tables

Acknowledgments

The question of media bias is one on which a great many people have opinions and very few have the discipline and training to get past their subjective impressions. There have been a number of people—their works are cited in Appendix A—who have done so. The nature of meta-analysis is that it stands, even more than the usual work of social science, on the shoulders of others; this report could not have been produced if they had not done the long and difficult work they have done.

I must also recognize that the lion's share of work that became this book was possible due to a sabbatical leave from the University of Connecticut. Those of us who practice the social sciences from the realms of academe are used to the many demands on our time, but the freedom to simply research, think, and write is invaluable.

As the process of publishing this book draws to a conclusion, I have to thank the people at Lexington Press. They have done a great job dealing with a cranky, bald, old coot.

That leaves four people who need specific mention. The first is Mike Allen, who has been a better friend and collaborator than I deserve through the years. His Brewers are playing well as I type this.

Guido Stempel commented extensively on a draft of this book and his feedback has been not only a great help but also a great source of pride to me. When people argue with me I remind them I have been researching this stuff for a decade; Professor Stempel has been researching this stuff for half a century.

Finally, there are my mother, Helen, and my late father, John. They taught me to think for myself and made it possible for me to be in a position in life to do exactly that. I would like to say there was no greater gift they could have given me, but there was: they also gave me a parent's love for their child, which is the pearl beyond price.

1

On the Nature of Media Bias

The candidate was up all night with his aides, tracking the returns, counting the votes, and increasingly hoping against hope that by morning the votes would be there for him to be elected governor of California. They were not. He lost and it was time for him to concede the election.

The reporters, gathered in the Cadoro room of the Beverly Hilton in Los Angeles, were told to expect a short statement from the campaign's press secretary, Herb Klein. Once the statement was finished, however, the candidate came out and spoke directly to the press corps himself. In the course of the next sixteen minutes and thirty-eight seconds Richard Nixon delivered one of the most remarkable statements in American political history.

The best-known line: "You won't have Nixon to kick around anymore, because, gentlemen, this is my last press conference . . ." proved prophetically true but in a way no one ever expected. As Joe McGinnis was to show in *The Selling of the President 1968*, in the last chapter of his political life Nixon simply stopped having any sort of dialog with the press (McGinnis, 1969), and so, in a way, that morning in 1962 in the Beverly Hilton truly was his last press conference.

But the transcript (*New York Times*, 1962) and audio recording of the press conference, readily available for download on the Internet (History Channel, 2008), remain remarkable documents. Nixon's tone is flat, his words in places apologetic. He does not sound as though he is berating or browbeating; his tone is simply that of an outsider telling the reporters about what he saw and how he saw it.

Browbeating he is, of course. Nixon later claimed he had not intended to address the press, but as he and his team watched Klein address the conference, they saw the reporters laughing and jeering. (Other observers do not recall this happening.) Staffer H. R. Haldeman reportedly said, "They should be told just where the hell to get off," (cited in Ambrose, 1987, p. 669), and the candidate went in to do just that.

He opened by congratulating the victor, Pat Brown, in a backhanded way: "I believe Governor Brown has a heart, even though he believes I do not. I believe he is a good American, even though he feels I am not." He thanked the 100,000 volunteers who worked on his campaign. He discussed the international political scene, dominated at that time by President Kennedy's handling of the Bay of Pigs fiasco, the abortive invasion of Cuba by Cuban émigrés trained and supported by the CIA with the aim of overthrowing the Castro regime. He discussed the election returns from around the nation: Republican gains in the House, the victories of Rockefeller in New York and Romney in Michigan and what they presaged for the 1964 presidential campaign. He talked about his personal plans.

And he said, "I did not win. I have no hard feelings against anybody . . ." but the rest of his words belie that claim. Richard Nixon looked political oblivion square in the face: his rivals in the party (Rockefeller and Romney) were winners and he a loser. Worse, he predicted, in a letter to former President Eisenhower before he'd decided to run, that "If I were to lose, I could be finished as far as public influence is concerned," (Ambrose, 1987, p. 646) and he did lose. He clearly felt the press corps cheated him during the campaign, regardless of their actual performance, and this is apparent throughout the transcript. David Halberstam's (1979) opinion on this moment is that, having lost, Nixon needed someone to blame for the losses in 1960 and then 1962, and since his personal self-image did not permit the losses to be his fault or the failing of his personal beliefs, it must have been someone else's, and here in the Beverly Hilton his eyes were firmly on the press.

Nixon, after his opening remarks, started discussing the press: "I appreciate the press coverage in this campaign. . . . I have no complaints about the press coverage," he said, but in fact, he did have complaints, and he returned to them again and again. He made explicit that he was displeased that certain stories hadn't played the way he'd wanted them played: "I am proud that I defended my opponent's patriotism. You gentlemen didn't report it, but I am proud that I did that. . . . I would appreciate if you would write what I say, in that respect. I think it's very important that you write it—in the lead . . . " He called out one reporter by name, Carl Thompson of the *Los Angeles Times*, to commend him for his objectivity, managing to imply the entire remainder of the press corps had not been objective. He was irritated that he had made a mistake—at one point said he was running for "Governor of the United States of America"—and it was reported (by the *Los Angeles Times*), while Governor Brown made a mistake (describing then-Senator Thomas Kuchel as a member of the Democratic ticket when Kuchel had been a lifelong moderate Republican) and Brown's mistake was not reported. The idea that Brown's comment might have been a bit facetious, and meant to indicate his association with a moderate Republican, does not appear to have occurred to Nixon, who was notorious for lacking a sense of humor (Ambrose, 1987).

Even as he berated the press for not reporting exactly what he wanted reported exactly the way he wanted it reported, he also berated them for their lack of objectivity: "Never in my 16 years of campaigning have I complained to a publisher, to an editor, about the coverage of a reporter. . . . I will say to the reporter sometimes that I think, look, I wish you'd give my opponent the same going over that you give me," and "I think it's time that our great newspapers have at least the same objectivity, the same fullness of coverage, that television has. And I can only say thank God for television and radio for keeping the newspapers a little more honest . . . The great metropolitan newspapers in this field, they have a right to take every position they want on the editorial page but on the news page they also have a right to have reporters (who) will at least report what the man says."

The clearest outcome of this performance is the model of the candidate as commodity that has overtaken American politics in the twenty-first century. There is obviously an adversarial relationship between candidates and the press and, following and based on Nixon's successful comeback campaign in 1968 and the methods deployed by his handlers, there is clearly the idea among politicians that the press exists to be managed to meet the interests of the candidate rather than the public. But this is discussed at great length elsewhere (c.f. Jamieson, 2006).

ABOUT THIS BOOK

I intend this book to be a lengthy analysis of media bias in the coverage of presidential election campaigns, its geneses, valences and magnitudes. As a social scientist rather than politician or journalist I intend to use the methods of social science to discover the answers to questions rather than deciding a priori what the answers are and then "proving" whether they are true.

From the perspective of a social scientist there are two great ironies in Nixon's accusations. The first is that he is demonstrably wrong. In singling out the *Los Angeles Times*, for instance, he reveals more about his mental processes and the mental processes of politicians than he reveals about media biases for or against candidates. The *Times*, as it happens, was enormously invested in ensuring its news coverage of the 1962 campaign for governor of California was as fair and balanced toward both major party candidates as was humanly possible. Two editors were assigned to monitor the *Times'* coverage, to ensure to the best of their ability that the campaigns were covered equally in both the number and length of story (volume of coverage) and also in tone (or valence). The *Times* even rotated its main correspondents from one campaign to the other, so whatever individual differences there were between reporters would be spread equally among the campaigns. Halberstam's conclusion seems apt: "The truth was that the reporting on his and Pat Brown's race was fair and balanced, what every politician hopes to get from the major metropolitan paper, a fair break and a decent hearing" (p. 349). Similarly, Ambrose (1987) concluded, "In the judgment of this author, the reporters and their publishers were highly professional" (p. 664). Yet, ironically, Nixon thought the *Times*, and the other news media outlets, had stuck it to him (Nixon, 1978; Halberstam, 1979).

And the second great irony is simply that, because of the past behavior of the *Los Angeles Times,* Nixon had a certain right to feel as though he had been mistreated. According to Halberstam (1979), the *Los Angeles Times* had been a Republican paper for decades: it was anti-union, pro-business, anti–New Deal and anti-communist throughout its days. In 1946 it was *Los Angeles Times* political reporter Kyle Palmer who had been actively looking for someone to oppose their Democratic then-congressman Jerry Voorhis and had discovered the modest Navy veteran and fervent anti-communist who was Richard Milhous Nixon. It was the *Times* that put him up to running and supported his campaign with totally one-sided news and editorial coverage. When it was time to run against Clare Booth Luce for U.S. Senate Nixon was the *Los Angeles Times'* boy, and the *Times'* coverage of the 1952 Eisenhower/Nixon tandem for president/vice president largely swamped that accorded their Democratic opponents in both volume and tone (Blumberg, 1954). The *Times'* coverage was also much stronger for Nixon than Kennedy in the 1960 presidential race (Stempel, 1961). But in 1962, all of a sudden, Nixon was not the *Times'* man . . . of course it seemed unfair and a betrayal to him—it was completely unprecedented and unexpected. And in fact, one of the things Nixon complained of the most is not that the press was not objective, but that they didn't tell him they were going to have the biases he perceived in them. "I want newspapers . . . ," he told the gathered reporters, pausing to construct his thoughts before going on, "If they're against a candidate I want them to say it" (*New York Times*, 1962).

In Nixon's press conference and the years of events that preceded it and followed from it we see a number of themes I intend to introduce, which are key to understanding the discussions that surround the topic of media bias.

* First, the perception of media bias by individual persons is subjective and so individual claims of bias must be treated with healthy skepticism.

* Second, the evidence that people commonly cite as proof of bias often fail to provide an adequate basis for a conclusion of bias.
* Third, the sources of systematic variations in coverage, including biases, are varied and not simply grounded in partisan or ideological beliefs of people associated with news media outlets.
* Fourth, working journalists act as though the opposite of biased coverage is balanced coverage.
* Fifth, there is a distinction between opinion-based content and news content.

I will discuss each of these items in turn, but first: Exactly what is media bias, and why should anyone care about it?

THE NATURE OF MEDIA BIAS

Political actors and commentators who routinely express their opinions of the existence, magnitude and valence of anything they term "media bias" rarely take the time to explain what they are talking about. This is almost certainly not an accident. Many discussions of media bias are based less on the desire for the American citizenry to be fully informed about the nature of bias and more on the need for the commentator to score points for his or her side in whatever argument he or she is making. If the term is undefined then anything can be "bias" and the argument is won. From that it follows that, once anything can be evidence of bias, then everything can be evidence of bias. Even, as in Nixon's case in 1962, the lack of bias can be regarded as evidence of bias.

Gerald Miller and Henry Nicholson (1976) have discussed the critical importance of the definition of terms. They point out that a quality definition performs not one but several tasks. A definition contains a composition description, for instance, which is what one typically thinks of in a definition: a set of terms that create a semantic equivalent for the term under discussion. But a definition also defines boundary conditions. All objects that fit the definition are describable by the term defined, but also any object that fails to meet the terms of the definition is excluded. It is also valuable that a definition reflect previous usage. Toward that end it is necessary to consider the nature of the idea of media bias in some depth in order to define the term "media bias."

In formal scientific terms, a bias is a systematic deflection from accuracy in the measurement of some quantity. The notion is explicitly embedded in all sorts of measurement instruments such as spectrometers and the like. As an example, a digital scale used for weighing chemicals in a laboratory will often have a "tare" button that automatically subtracts the weight of the container. The empty container is placed on the scale, the scale "tared" to make the weight of the container known, the container filled, and then weighed again, with the scale automatically subtracting the weight of the container so that the weight of the chemical is known. In the absence of taring, the weight of the container would bias the measurement of the weight of chemical upward.

For our purposes, "bias" is of necessity a more complex concept. "What quantity of chemical do I have?" is a very different question than "What quantity of fairness do I have?" Nonetheless, a formal definition of media bias has to encompass the essence of the scientific nature of a bias, that of a systematic deflection.

Media systems in some European nations are operated essentially as public trusts, and as such are expected as a matter of course to report news stories objectively (c.f. Gunther, 1997). Although it is arguable whether a single reporter or even an entire news organization can be truly objective, the fact remains that news objectivity is explicitly a goal state to be striven for in these countries. As a consequence, at times researchers are commissioned to examine the handling of certain stories to make evaluations of the performance of news media. Researchers tasked with evaluating the performance of news media in Sweden and the UK (Westerstahl, 1983; Gunter, 1997) have generally conceptualized objectivity as encompassing the concepts of factuality and impartiality. They consider factuality to be based on whether the facts presented in reporting the story are both true and also relevant. Impartiality demands that reporting be balanced, meaning that all significant viewpoints are represented roughly equally, and that the information is presented as being impartial in tone. Note that the latter two are the same criteria adopted by the *Los Angeles Times* in its coverage of the Nixon/Brown gubernatorial race. The obvious implication of this approach is that if objectivity is the goal state, then bias can be conceptualized as a departure from objectivity.

In the United States the first formal examinations of media bias were made as a response to the virulent charges made by President Harry S Truman and the supporters of Democratic presidential candidate Adlai Stevenson that the news media of 1952 constituted a "One Party Press" (*The New York Times,* 1952. In fact, Truman had started hammering out this theme in his 1948 campaign, claiming that 90 percent of the editorial pages of newspapers supported his opponent, Thomas Dewey, although analysis shows the figure was closer to 65 percent; Ross, 1968). Researchers had measured coverage of presidential elections previous to the 1952 campaign (e.g. Berelson, Lazarsfeld & McPhee, 1954), but not in the context of examining partisan biases in reporting. These earliest studies of bias per se, such as those conducted by Blumberg (1954) and Kobre (1953) made no attempt to explicitly define bias but, by counting elements such as the number of stories about each campaign or the number of photographs of each candidate, created an implicit definition that bias is demonstrated by an imbalance in the amount of coverage (although Blumberg also recorded his subjective impression of the tone of a newspaper's stories in a non-numerical way). When Klein and Maccoby (1954) did explicitly define bias, it was specifically as an operationalization: "'Bias' is here defined as the existence of a differential, larger than could be expected by chance alone, between the proportional front-page coverage allotted the two candidates by the two sets of papers," comprising the sample (p. 289). Their focus on front-page coverage was made for the purpose of ease of measurement, but the idea of balance as a nonsignificant difference in proportion of coverage is illuminating.

The attacks on the media undertaken by then–Vice President Spiro Agnew in the late 1960s (Agnew, 1969a; Agnew, 1969b) engendered a second round of formal and informal studies of news content from the standpoint of its ideological bias (or lack thereof). Again, as was the case in the first round of studies, in many of these reports bias is simply undefined and is implied by the existence of an unbalance in news coverage.

Defining Media Bias

In his attempt to reconcile the grossly different conclusions drawn by previous critics such as Efron (1971), Epstein (1973) and Lefever (1974), Alden Williams (1975) first attempted to consider the nature and characteristics of media bias in formal terms, in order to create some form of larger conceptionalization of what the term means. His glib definition, "bias . . . (is) properly thought of as deviation from an unattainable but theoretically conceivable condition of unbias . . ." (p. 191) is of little use. In the formal terms of logic, his claim is essentially that "biased," means "not unbiased." But if bias is the state of "not unbiased," what does "unbiased" mean?

Far more importantly, Williams outlined four characteristics that needed to be displayed in order to make an observed bias in television news (his discussion was specific to network television news, but is more widely applicable) "remarkable":

> First, to be remarkable, bias must be volitional. If it is beyond an act of will, of intellect, or of the community to change, whether "knowing" bias or not, it is not likely to be widely interesting. Second, remarkable bias must be putatively influential; bias behavior without purpose is either unremarkable or dull. Third, remarkable bias must be reasonably, plausibly threatening to conventional

values or institutions; extreme biases of half-wits and knaves may not be dull, but they are not threatening either. Fourth, remarkable bias is sustained, not one-shot. It must last, or promise to last, long enough to be effective. (p. 192)

By "remarkable bias" it is clear that Williams intends to mean biases that are subject to remark because of their potential to influence the political life of the community, nation or world, of which there are potentially many. Page and Shapiro (1992) have discussed no fewer than eight types of bias in American media: anti-communist, minimal government, nationalistic, ethnocentric, partisan, pro-incumbent, pro-status quo and pro-capitalist. Of these, most are literally unremarkable because they are essentially transparent to mainstream American thought. For instance, it is self-evident that American news media are nationalistic: it is their function to attract readers and viewers in America, so it is necessary that they focus their attentions on America and Americans. Similarly, Gans (1979) discussed a consistent bias toward ethnocentrism as well, plus biases toward holding democracy to be altruistic, capitalism to be responsible (as opposed to generally irresponsible), and treating small-town pastoralism, moderation and individualism as good. Again, to mainstream American thought these values tend to be transparent.

The most remarkable sort of bias, to use Williams' term, is partisan bias, the favoritism on the part of the media for one party's positions over the other's. This is held to be closely related to a form of bias not listed by Page and Shapiro, that being ideological bias, the preference for one end or the other of the conservative/liberal continuum. Partisan and ideological biases are frequently mistaken for one another because of the general association of Democrat politicians with liberal ideologies and Republicans with conservative ones, but it is worth noting that in the case of individual politicians and individual issues these associations may be incorrect or may change over time.

As we have seen, Williams has described remarkable bias as both volitional and threatening to conventional values. It should be noted that the volition involved can come from anywhere in the media system and not necessarily the writer/creator/presenter of the news in question. In chapter 2 there is a discussion of the kinds of biases that are manifest in American news media and their geneses in the nature of the industry and the sorts of people involved with it. And, of course, the conventional values being threatened can include beliefs associated with broadly held ideological positions; for instance, the desirability of the legality or prohibition of same-sex marriages. As will be seen in chapter 3, it is possible for a neutral, fair and balanced story on such a controversial topic to be considered as threatening by holders of either position.

Williams' third descriptor, that remarkable bias be putatively, or potentially, influential is worth noting in passing in that it is self-evident. If news media were not putatively influential there would be no discussion of their content.

It seems evident that the last of Williams' requirements, that bias be sustained, is one of the critical issues in the examination of bias. An entity that is sustained, as Williams has used the term, is also systematic in the scientific sense discussed previously. It is one thing to point at a single story and claim that the story is biased. It is a simple matter, and in fact probably common, for a given single report to be one-sided in that deadline pressures can force the story into the public's eye before the other side of the story can be reached for reply. It is another thing entirely to claim that a reporter or a news outlet is biased because a single story is biased. In formal terms, to do so is to argue inductively from a single case. Such arguments are false as often as they are true; they are the logical equivalent of projecting a series of coin flips based on only the first. To avoid drawing false conclusions from the happenstance of daily news gathering, favoritism of any kind must be systematic or sustained (as Williams would say), for one to be able to reach the reasonable conclusion that the reporter or the outlet is biased.

As an aside, this is one of the mistakes Nixon makes in his news conference. He believes that the *Los Angeles Times* is trying to "get him" because they report an error of fact he makes (misstating that he is running for "governor of the United States") and not one that his opponent makes (misidentifying Tom Kuchel as a Democrat). In this case he looks at a single instance of reporting and reaches a conclusion about the aggregate of news coverage. As we will see in chapter 3, this is exactly the way many people observe "bias" in the media: they focus on isolated instances and draw unwarranted conclusions from them.

It is also worth noting at this time that observers at the time drew an important distinction between the two errors of fact. There was nothing to indicate that Governor Brown's mistaken reference to Senator Kuchel's party affiliation was anything more than an accident, if not even a joke. However, contemporary observers were concerned that Nixon's campaign was diffuse and lacking in direction, and had reached the conclusion that his heart was not really in the campaign for governor because governor of California was not the office he really wanted, a conclusion which was valid—see Nixon (1978). The press and observers believed that Nixon, having lost his race for the presidency in 1960, was still looking forward to the White House, which he indeed achieved in 1968, that his slip of the tongue was an external manifestation of that goal, and consequently that knowledge of it would be useful to the electorate.

Two formal definitions of media bias have drawn on the concept of a bias being "sustained" (in Williams' terms) as being the critical element of the notion of bias. Theoretician Denis McQuail called media bias a "consistent deviation in a particular direction." (1987, p. 167) This includes the fundamental scientific notion of a bias being a systematic deflection from a goal state, and in fact McQuail implies the goal state of media coverage. If bias is a tendency to favor one side or the other systematically, then an unbiased position is one in which the coverage on the whole (or in the aggregate) favors neither.

Later this definition was extended to include the concepts Williams termed "volitional" and "influential": bias is "a systematic, persistent unbalance in mainstream news coverage for the purpose of influencing opinion on key issues." (D'Alessio & Allen, 2006, p. 432). This definition subsumes the key concepts from Williams' work into a single statement, and gives us a sense for what can reasonably be described as "biased" or "unbiased." For instance, no single story or news item in and of itself can be regarded as proof of bias, and in fact no arbitrary sample drawn non-randomly from a body of content should be sufficient to reach that conclusion, either. As we will see in chapter 3 it is common for critics to pick out a series of items from an entire body of work, ignoring and excluding the others, in order to submit the selected items as proof of bias. But to demonstrate that a body of work shows unbalances that are both persistent and systematic, one has to look at the entire body of work, or a randomly sampled subset of it, and find aggregate unbalances in the whole or subset.

This definition also limits discussion to the mainstream media simply because it is the mainstream media that are expected to be "influential," to use Williams' term. Put simply, fringe media are attended by only a small number of users, and in the political sense they contribute little to the swaying of mass opinion. Finally, the notion of balance was chosen as the goal state of media from which persistent deflections will be described as biases. This was done to take into account existing international standards, as Westerstahl has laid them out, as well as the goals of the journalistic profession itself. As we will see, balance is one of the goals that journalism has set for itself, and is the appropriate goal for media to be judged by in this regard.

THE DIFFICULTY OF BEING UNBIASED

Although the goal state of balanced coverage seems straightforward, the mechanics of the news-gathering process makes it difficult to achieve under ordinary circumstances, particularly in the short-term time frame of the daily news cycle. While certain elements of any news story can reasonably be identified as factual—"who," "what," "where" and "when" are often things on which complete agreement should be reached—beyond those simple items media critics claim that objectivity, and by implication balance, is impossible. The reason for this is that beyond the simple, basic facts of a given situation, information concerning an event starts to reach an amount that is unmanageable in its entirety. There is simply too much information in a given news situation for a newspaper to profitably include all of it in the published report of the situation. Consequently, decisions have to be made about which pieces of information will be included and which excluded. A good example is the news report in *The New York Times* of Nixon's 1962 concession press conference (Hill, 1962). The news report draws from the transcript the concession itself, the attack on the press, and no more than one or two more of the other points. Had the *Times* not found the room to publish the entire transcript elsewhere on the page, the isolated points recorded in the news report would have been the only points the reading audience would have been aware of.

Lester Markel of *The New York Times* summarized the problem of selecting information for publication elegantly:

> The reporter, the most objective reporter, collects fifty facts. Out of the fifty he selects twelve to include in his story (there is such a thing as space limitation). Thus he discards thirty-eight. This is Judgment Number One.
>
> Then the reporter or the editor decides which of the facts shall be in the first paragraph of the story, thus emphasizing one fact over the other eleven. This is Judgment Number Two.
>
> Then the editor decides whether the story shall be placed on Page One or Page Twelve; on Page One it will command many times the attention it would on Page Twelve. This is Judgment Number Three.
>
> The so-called factual presentation is thus subjected to three judgments, all of them humanly and most ungodly made. (Cited in quotation by Rivers, 1965, p. 43)

Markel's point is, of course, that where human judgment is involved, any number of criteria, including but not limited to personal values, may come into play. As Bagdikian (1971) and White (1950) have noted, the speed at which these judgments are made magnifies the problem. White's study is of particular value here. He simply watched over the shoulder of the wire-services editor of a newspaper as the editor selected—and rejected—stories for the day's paper, and had the editor comment briefly on each. Indeed, while looking over the shoulder of his pseudonymous Mr. Gates, White did observe that some of the judgments were made for reasons of personal ideology.

A news medium that is to be described as "unbiased," therefore, will have to make a deliberate attempt to balance its coverage of an issue. This is not something that happens often by accident or random chance simply because of the number of subjective decisions that must be made in the course of gathering news and presenting it to the public. Instead, it has to be approached systematically in some way.

The problem of ensuring that news coverage is balanced is enormously magnified by the fact that the notion of "news" itself is ill-defined. Gerald Johnson, the respected *Baltimore Sun* columnist and journalism professor, described news as, essentially, that which gives a first-rate journalist satisfaction to report (Johnson, 1926). This was done almost a century ago, but Johnson's description is still held to have a certain degree of validity. It is misquoted, for instance, in *The New News Business*, the guide to writing and reporting news assembled by longtime NBC news anchor John Chancellor and Associated Press vice president Walter Mears (Chancellor & Mears, 1995).

Other perspectives include the concept of public interest as part of the concept of news. Peter Mayeaux's (1996) textbook described news as "what people need and want to know" (p. 4), pointing out that it should contain some combination of characteristics including proximity, prominence, timeliness, impact, conflict, controversy, uniqueness, human interest, suspense, updating and availability of sound and pictures. The judgments of whether the people need or want to know something, and whether the story is proximate, timely or suspenseful is left to the editor(s) and writer(s) in question.

The ambiguity regarding the nature of news extends from not just journalists but to news organizations as well. The *Associated Press Reporting Handbook* (Schwartz, 2002) implies that news is what, in a reporter's judgment, the reader might be interested in. The author, Jerry Schwartz, quotes then-AP president and CEO Louis Boccardi as saying news is "anything that will make anyone say 'my my'" (p. 22). The *Scripps-Howard Handbook* (Trimble, 1948/1981), assembled to orient newcomers to the organization and practices of the Scripps-Howard chain, makes it a point to say that the concept "news" is hard to define (albeit easier to recognize), and gives a series of abstract examples: "News is something unusual or fantastic or bizarre . . . news is a contest between men, or between men and nature . . . News is a description of what men pay for and women wear . . . " (p. 25). In essence, news is a good story, for any one of a number of given values of "good."

This definitional ambiguity leaves journalism unprotected against charges of bias. It is a simple conclusion to reach that if the only thing that determines the newsworthiness of an item are the opinions of the concerned writer and editor, then the news will be suffused with the personal opinions and beliefs of newsmen, who are, in the main, politically to the left. This is exactly the conclusion reached by a number of critics attempting to "prove" that the media are biased (e.g. Dautrich & Hartley, 1999; Bozell & Baker, 1990).

An appropriate response, of course, is that the audience constitutes a suitable preventative against this. A journalist could argue, reasonably, that the audience has the final approval over the content of any news medium; that they can vote with their purchase and consumption decisions on the type and quality of news presented to them. This is explicit in the history of the Associated Press. The *Associated Press Reporting Handbook* (Schwartz, 2002) quotes AP's first Washington correspondent, Lawrence Gobright, who stated explicitly, "My business is to communicate facts. . . . My instructions do not allow me to make any comment upon the facts. My dispatches are sent to papers of all manners of politics. I therefore confine myself to what I consider legitimate news and try to be truthful and impartial." It has to be recognized that, at some level, virtually all U.S. news outlets are commercial entities that are supported by their users, whether it be by subscription or by delivering the subscriber's eyes to advertisers, and that news outlets that sufficiently outrage their users will drive them off, rendering the outlet commercially unviable.

As we will see, however, this economic evaluation implies the possibility that business decisions have the capability to impact news content and news coverage systematically just as a reporter's personal prejudices might, which is to say, they could act as a source of bias in media reports. And, indeed, we will see that the complex sociological nature of media industries has the potential to create any of a number of preferences in the enormous number of decisions that the members of the news organization have to make every day in deciding what is news and how the news is to be told.

THE IMPORTANCE OF UNBIASED NEWS

Evaluating the number, types and valences of potential biases in the news should be of value to the advancement of democracy and democratic dialog as we understand those ideas. If Thomas Jefferson's observation that "the tree of liberty must be refreshed from time to time with the blood of patriots and tyrants" is true, then it is equally true that the great forest that is representative democracy as practiced in the United States must delve its roots deeply into the vast reservoir that is information. The flow of information, from electorate to elected and back, is critical to the functioning of a representative democracy, as it is critical for representatives to have knowledge of the will of the electorate, and the electorate to have knowledge of the behavior of its representatives (c.f. Meiklejohn, 1948; Lippmann, 1922/1991).

Not only is an unbiased news flow philosophically critical to a representative democracy, there is some empirical evidence suggesting that biased news flows have consequential impacts on voting behavior. Experiments involving news material deliberately biased for experimental purposes show that participants reported altered voting preferences after reading biased newspaper articles (Hoffman & Wallach, 2007) and watching biased TV reports, particularly reports whose tone or manner of speaking is biased (Norris & Sanders, 1998). Similarly, candidates who were seen facing hostile interviewers (Babad, 2005) were evaluated more poorly. Results from field studies indicate that readers of a liberally biased local daily newspaper were more likely to vote for the Democratic candidate in a Senate election than the readers of a centrist local newspaper (Druckman & Parkin, 2005). And DellaVigna and Kaplan (2007) showed that local communities gaining access to the presumably conservative Fox News channel for the first time had a small but measurable tendency toward yielding larger numbers of Republican votes in the next election, even following application of multiple statistical controls.

None of these studies constitutes the "smoking gun" that would constitute proof that news media influence voting. The experimental studies are potentially subject to demand effects: for instance, it is simple for a cooperative experimental participant to read a negative article about a candidate and conclude that the researcher "wanted" a negative evaluation of the candidate. Druckman and Parkin have overlooked the fact that liberal voters are more likely to be attracted to a liberal newspaper—in fact, in chapter 2 it will be shown that this is an economic justification for biased media—and thus the association between reading liberal and voting Democratic is not clear evidence of a causal link running from the media to voting patterns (*see* Cook & Campbell, 1979); instead, both are indicators of being liberal in worldview. DellaVigna and Kaplan (2007) do not distinguish between Fox News channel's news reporting, which may or may not be biased, from the channel's opinion and commentary materials, which are undoubtedly conservative.

However, the consistency of results across each of these studies is very high. In each case, voting evaluations were associated with biased news reports or news channels, and more importantly, the association was positive. The report and the evaluation were each valenced in the same direction, regardless of whether that direction was liberal/Democratic or conservative/Republican. Certainly the results show that biased news can potentially influence voting: there is no evidence of a failure to influence.

In principle, the electorate can come to know its potential representatives by meeting and talking with them; by listening to them speak, and watching and reading their advertisements; by reading their position papers; by consulting their Web sites; by talking to people that know them; by enjoying their appearances on David Letterman or *The Daily Show*; and by following the progress of their campaigns in news reports appearing on television and in newspapers. Of all these general classes of media outlet, however, only one is charged with the obligation of objectivity: the news. And that makes it necessary to consider the nature of the news industries of the United States, in order to uncover systemic elements that can systematically influence news decisions, thereby creating biases. Chapter 2 will approach this subject in depth.

Recognition of the unique mandate that news media have in serving their users, themselves and the political process also requires that this study be limited, and limited carefully, to news reportage. Most news outlets provide commentary, editorial and opinion material provided by in-house commentators and editors, syndication, and even members of the general public. This is a very broad potential menu of thoughts and ideas: there is not even the requirement that writers of letters to the editors of newspapers actually read the newspaper in question. These materials are specifically not news and are generally not identified as such; their function is to articulate positions on issues. In many cases—as examples, Jon Stewart, Sean Hannity, Rush Limbaugh and Al Franken—the presenters are not journalists, have little or no journalistic training and no professional mandate to adhere to the ethical codes of journalism. It is not their purpose or their function to provide factually based, balanced, unbiased information. As a rule their material is presented separately from a news outlet's news content, on a separate TV or radio show or on the op-ed pages of the newspaper, and is often labeled explicitly as opinion. It is possible that that such material is influential, and Mankiewicz (1989) has suggested that it is. Indeed, there is an entire literature on the subject of the leading of mass opinion by influential individuals (e.g., Katz & Lazarsfeld, 1955). But it is not news reporting, and so the question as to whether it is biased is moot. It is opinion and everyone is entitled to their opinions.

In this study I am going to focus on the concept of media bias as it occurs in the context of presidential election campaigns. There are a number of reasons for this decision. Firstly, the choice of a president every four years is probably the most important political decision that the American populace regularly makes. The media, and the news media in particular, play a critical role in this process. The U.S. electorate is simply too large for every voter to have some kind of firsthand experience with the candidates, and in the absence of physical contact, the electorate must receive mediated material. There are a great many sources of information, but, as we have seen, of them only the news reports in the news media are not explicitly or implicitly self-serving toward the needs of the candidates or other entities engaged in the campaign.

Secondly, it is the candidates themselves who have created the perception that the idea of media bias is worthy of comment. George H. W. Bush's campaign circulated the popular bumper sticker that said, "Annoy the Media: Re-elect Bush," but Bush was neither the first nor the last candidate to complain about the nature of his coverage. Nor were the points raised by Nixon in 1962 the first time they had been heard. Adlai Stevenson's and Spiro Agnew's complaints were not the only ones made in the 1950s and 1960s; the media have been a constant whipping boy for the last four and a half decades. And as recently as the Democratic nominating campaign of 2008 one candidate made public complaints about the media favoring her opponent. But Harry Truman was not the first candidate to complain, nor will Hillary Clinton be the last. It is simpler to believe (and to act on the belief) that "the media are out to get me" than to believe "I am wrong" for many candidates.

Thirdly, because complaints made by presidential candidates have brought the question of media bias to public prominence, the importance of the question has led to a research agenda that emphasizes examination of media coverage of presidential campaigns. There have been formal studies of the degree to which media content is or is not biased on issues of race (Martindale, 1985; Niven, 2002), gender (Silver, 1986; Smith, 1997; Davis, 1982) and nationality (Paraschos & Rutherford, 1985; Barranco & Shyles, 1988), and for a number of election campaigns conducted for gubernatorial, House and/or Senate seats (for example, Markham, 1961; Carter, Fico & McCabe, 2002; Barrett & Barrington, 2005; and Schiffer, 2006, among many others). But there is probably a larger body of published research on the coverage of presidential election campaigns than of all those other issues and elections combined. The chosen method of analysis chosen for this study is meta-analysis (see chapter 3), and for meta-analytic purposes the larger the number of studies available for analysis and summary, the clearer, stronger, more detailed and more useful the final conclusions.

Finally, from a strictly pragmatic standpoint, a presidential campaign has the structural advantage that the point at which coverage can be said to be balanced is relatively easy to determine. Two candidates, each nominated by one of the two parties that has supplied every president since the mid-1800s, and in fact since World War II supplied them on a regularly alternating eight-year cycle (with the exception of 1980–1984), suggests that the parties themselves are fairly well balanced and that coverage of them should be split fairly close to evenly. (This may not always be the case, however, and there are other approaches to this question that will be addressed in chapter 3.)

In chapter 2 we will examine the nature of news media in the United States. The tension between news organizations as professional entities and as profit-making businesses has been commented on extensively, and, in addition they are also both the property of a person or company and actors in the political process in their own rights. The needs of each of these separate identities each have the potential to create biases of various sorts in news reporting; some of these biases may be either overtly partisan or ideological and some may create in turn positions associated with ideological positions.

The methodology will be laid out in chapter 3. The subjective nature of perceptions of media bias will be discussed, and as a result the measurement of bias requires measurement techniques that formally act to remove or mitigate subjective judgments, typically the use of content analysis. To this end we have gathered a large database of content analyses with the intention of aggregating them using meta-analytic techniques, and so in chapter 3 we will also describe how meta-analysis is performed and how meta-analytic results are interpreted.

In chapters 4 and 5 we will present the results of the meta-analyses conducted for this book. Chapter 4 tackles the large questions: are the media (in the aggregate, as a group) biased in the way that critics and politicians claim? Is there are an overall liberal bias? An overall conservative bias? Do the newspaper and TV industries differ? Chapter 5 will consider the questions raised by the analysis of the news media industries discussed in chapter 2 by considering media outlets as individual entities with different ownerships. Regardless of whether the media in the aggregate are liberal, conservative or neither, it should be obvious that the content of certain individual outlets differs ideologically from others. For instance, it is well established that the news content of the *Washington Times* is politically further to the right than that of the *Washington Post* (Kenney & Simpson, 1993). This statement is true regardless of whether one, the other or both are or are not ideologically biased. One or the other may be unbiased but they cannot both be because on the whole their ideologies are manifestly different. Are there systematic regularities in the socioeconomic circumstances of different media outlets that are associated with content to the left, right or center ideologically?

Finally, chapter 6 will take a look at what the findings are and try to place them into the larger context of the political process.

2

Forces Acting on the News

The news media industries in the United States are probably in unique circumstances compared to those faced by any other socioeconomic entities in the nation. As we have already seen, the very notion of "news" as news people define it implies a degree of compromise between two competing industrial identities, between the idealistic profession of journalism and the needs and requirements of operating a business in the United States. Journalists understand that ultimately, to accomplish whatever goals they aspire to in their profession, they must attract subscribers and buyers, as well as eyeballs to see the advertisements (c.f. Gelb, 2003).

This dichotomy is in and of itself is not unique. Many professions—medicine and architecture to name two—are placed in the position of having to balance the needs of a professional calling and the needs of business. What makes news industries unique is that they are also characterized by at least two additional essential natures whose needs are also potentially reflected in their news content. Along with being professions and businesses, a newspaper or TV station is also property: it belongs to some person or some other entity that has the right to control and dispose of it as desired. And unlike your family dentist, for instance, the news media are also treated as and considered to be political entities, not in the narrow sense that they are elected or part of the electorate, but in the broad sense of contributing to and mediating the dialog through which the nation is governed.

NEWS AS A PROFESSION

As a rule, critics of the news media located ideologically on the conservative side of the spectrum point to the general tendency among news reporters to be

aligned ideologically with political liberalism. They point to polls of reporters in which the reporters polled report substantially larger tendencies to vote
Democratic than Republican, and offer them as the genesis for the belief that
"the media" (in the broadest possible terms) are liberal generally and that this
liberality is expressed in the content of media outlets. Few such critics claim
that this form of liberal bias is deliberate, but they argue that one's ideology
cannot help but creep into one's writing.

There is an element of truth underlying this position. Across four decades
Weaver and his colleagues (Weaver et al., 2007) have indeed shown that
journalists as a body are more likely to self-identify as leftist than rightist, and
more likely to self-identify as Democrat than Republican. The differences
are generally marked: identification with the political left has ranged from 38
percent to 49 percent of journalists; the right only 19 to 25 percent (with the
remainder centrist or not reporting). Similarly, support for the Democratic
party among working journalists ranges from 36 to 44 percent while 16 to
26 percent support the Republican party. Weaver and his co-workers have
repeated their surveys every ten years since the early 1970s, and while the
overall numbers can vary from decade to decade, the same pattern of support
for the left and for the Democrats shows up each time.

However, the argument that liberal reporters bias their reports liberally
is popular but at the same time an oversimplification so vast as to be disin-
genuous. To argue that "Reporters vote Democratic, so therefore they write
Democratic," for instance, implies that a reporter's political identity as a
voter is the single element of their being that is predominant in each of their
individual belief systems. It also ignores the extensive training the reporters
receive, and that their profession's professional standards call on them to be
fair, accurate and to show no favor. It also implies that reporters possess a
dominant position in the power structure of the newsroom, allowing them to
do as they please with no regard for the desires of their managers, for many of
the same polls show that the further up the organizational ladder of the news
media outlet one climbs, the more associated with the Republican Party one's
beliefs are. For instance, Mitchell (2000) showed that newspaper publishers
supported Bush over Gore in the 2000 campaign by almost a 3 to 1 margin,
59 percent to 20 percent (with most of the rest declining to respond).

These counterarguments are not based on mere speculation or special
pleading. Journalism texts (e.g., Mayeux, 1996) make it clear that fairness
and objectivity are expected of news reporting by users as a matter of course,
and the failure to be fair and objective is not only unethical but also results
in a loss of credibility. Schwartz (2002) has pointed out the potential economic consequences of the inability to be fair to the Associated Press. As a
consortium of currently about 1500 newspapers, the Associated Press must

serve outlets reflecting all sorts of ideology with the same stories. Consistent biases toward the left or the right would drive member papers with opposing ideologies out of the consortium, to its financial detriment. Former NBC news anchor John Chancellor (Chancellor & Mears, 1995) independently made exactly the same point.

Reporters themselves point out that they need to be aware of their personal preferences and suppress them in order to do their job properly. Johnson (1926) pointed out the ethical imperative involved: "A first-rate newspaperman . . . makes dispassionate, impartial judgments based on reason and experience, and on nothing else" (p. 90). Of course, this is a goal state rather than a claim that this state of affairs covers all reporters at all times; he makes no claim that all journalists are "first-rate." Patterson and Donsbach (1996) considered the matter empirically and concluded that "[Reporters'] partisan beliefs are clearly secondary to a professional orientation" (p. 466). Long-term Washington correspondent Helen Thomas (2006) evoked the old Scripps-Howard handbook from 1948: "We have no politics . . . We shall tell no lies about persons or policies for love or money" (p. 198).

Former AP vice president Walter Mears (Chancellor & Mears, 1995) discussed this at some length. He said,

> I'm often asked how it is possible to write about these things objectively when as a citizen I must have a preference for one candidate or the other. I reply that I have been trained, and have trained myself, not to let that be a factor in my work. In a campaign my job is to tell people—voters—everything I can about the candidates who want their support. If I can't do that fairly, I can't buy groceries or pay the rent. (p. 44)

So, while it is true that reporters have ideological values and beliefs, it is not necessarily true that it follows directly that those values and beliefs appear routinely in their news reports. Reporters are aware of their preferences and also for the need to be objective, and are capable of making a concerted effort to be fair and balanced. Indeed, Shoemaker and Reese (1996) cite the case of a reporter, who, on retrospection, felt that he had gone so far in the attempt to compensate for his personal preferences that he had actually gone too far and ended up appearing to advocate positions opposite his own.

In his ethnography of news media outlets, Herbert Gans (1979) concluded that in fact journalists tend to engage in value exclusion: they simply do not consider their own values while reporting, suppressing them for the purpose of "getting the story." Gans goes on to point out two mechanisms that support the process of value exclusion on the part of reporters. First, there are social pressures, up to and including reassignment, that are exerted on reporters who are perceived as being "too close" to their story, reminding them to distance themselves from it. Second, people who are overtly ideological and unwilling to exclude their own values from their reporting self-select out of journalistic positions. These mechanisms represent both external and internal pressures on the news reporter to achieve neutrality in reporting, regardless of individual ideology.

The organizational structure of a news media outlet as a hierarchy in which reporters are near the bottom also functions to regulate and suborn the opinions of individual reporters. In his examination of two newspapers notorious for partisan bias, Sigelman (1973) found there was neither an ideological test for hiring decisions nor a formal statement of, or training in, either paper's ideological position. However, it is nonetheless clear that social forces within the organizations acted so as to bring reporters' expressed opinions in line with those preferred at each paper. Sigelman observed socialization processes in place, an awareness on the part of reporters that they were expected to report as the boss liked ("He signs my check," according to one), and a tendency to self-select on the part of applicants, with rightist applicants applying to the rightist paper and leftists to the leftist. (Of course, reporters in these cases would be expressing their own views, but only because those views happened to coincide with those further up the hierarchy, which is to say, persons with more organizational power.) Additionally, Breed (1955) has pointed out that newspaper reporters routinely read the newspapers they work for daily. They can see for themselves patterns in editorial emendations to their stories and learn what to say in order to preclude editing. In this way, the political preferences of the paper are made manifest in the work of journalists who may or may not share those preferences.

On the whole, in the face of both professional values and on-site observations conducted by outsiders such as Gans and Sigelman, the notion that reporters routinely bend news to meet their ideological or partisan needs seems unlikely. However, the loose organizational structure of a news media outlet suggested by Sigelman allows a degree of leeway, and Patterson and Donsbach (1996) concluded that there is a small but measurable tendency for reporters to report from their own ideological perspective as such a loose structure would permit. Control originates in power, and power in management, but control of the newsroom is not absolute, potentially leaving some openings for a reporter's ideological preferences to shine through even as the overall policy is established higher up the corporate ladder.

THE IDEOLOGY OF JOURNALISM

There is some reason to expect news media to have specific biases associated with the political left not for ideological reasons but simply because in some ways journalistic values align themselves with values traditionally associated with liberalism (see Smith, 1990). Journalists tend to favor broad civil liberties, of course, because of the strong association between journalism and the First Amendment; they see threats against civil liberties as being threats against their livelihoods. Similarly, there is an industry-wide generalized preference for change rather than the status quo because in change there is conflict, in conflict drama, and in drama lies news.

It is important to note, on the other hand, that news values also align themselves with traditionally conservative values in other areas. The media tend to be anti-communist on the whole, for instance, communist nations being patent abusers of a free press, and generally prefer a looser regulatory environment, which makes news gathering and dissemination simpler and less expensive.

Other observers have noted that the needs of journalism as a profession lead to specific and measurable non-ideological biases in content. Reporters covering presidential election campaigns, for instance, have made the point that on a day-to-day basis a presidential candidate typically does very little that is newsworthy (c.f. Crouse, 1973; Thompson, 1973). On an average day the candidate will visit a number of locations and say basically the same thing at each (the "stump" speech), or else alter their standard address in order to emphasize points from their existing platforms most congenial to the specific audience they are addressing. (This can be seen explicitly at the beginning of *The Selling of the President* [McGinniss, 1969], as Richard Nixon records radio spot ads for his campaign.) The content of these speeches is rarely "new" and to a certain extent not newsworthy in the sense that it is something the audience can be presumed to already know.

On the other hand, the latest poll results or endorsements are "new," are material that is presumably not known to the audience, and are therefore "news." As a result, reporting tends to focus on the questions of "What do the polls say?" and "Who is ahead?" to the detriment of coverage of the issues. Patterson (1993), Littlewood (1999) and others have come to call this "Horse-Race Journalism," and it is a direct outcome of the need among news media outlets for news to be, in essence, "new."

Along with concerns that follow from the potential overuse of "horse-race" stories are those raised concerning the general negative tone of political campaign coverage. Lichter and his colleagues at the Center for Media and Public Affairs have documented that in the coverage of many recent presidential campaigns, negative coverage of candidates, regardless of party, outweighs coverage that is positive in tone (c.f. Farnsworth & Lichter, 2007). They, and other scholars such as Patterson (1993), are concerned with this phenomenon because they suspect that it contributes to the general cynicism of the American populace with political matters in general (and thus low turnouts at the polls and low levels of political knowledge among voters, each of which is an inefficiency in the proper functioning of a representative democracy).

Farnsworth and Lichter (2007) attribute the bias toward negative coverage to a generalized distrust of politicians that dates to the Watergate era, although they concede the possibility that it could go back further. An alternative explanation, of course, is the common journalistic notion that one of the proper functions of journalism is to perform an adversarial role, in order to watchdog the political process in the service of the public interest (c.f. Jefferson, 1787/2006; Schulte & DuFresne, 1994). In pointing out political fallacies and personal foibles that speak to the ability of certain candidates to perform in elected positions as part of their watchdog function, news media outlets of necessity produce material that is negative in tone. They would argue, quite reasonably, that to do otherwise would do a disservice to the voters. By simply presenting any information provided to them by candidates uncritically, news media outlets would be denying the electorate the resources and information it needs to critically evaluate campaign claims and promises.

It should be noted, of course, that a predominance of horse-race stories over issue-based reporting and of negatively toned material over positively toned material might constitute biases in news reporting that are based on the nature of news media as journalistic entities. There is no suggestion, however, that these biases are either partisan or ideological in nature in and of themselves, and as such they are beyond the scope of this book. If it is shown that coverage of one party is more negative than that of another on a consistent basis, however, that consistency could be evidence of partisan bias, as will be examined in chapter 3. But there is nothing inherent about these sorts of media bias that makes them partisan in nature.

Critics such as Lieberman (2000) and Cooper and Soley (1990) have argued, on the other hand, that the nature of journalistic storytelling, in which as a matter of course and of ethical practice a properly constructed news report tells both sides of a story, has opened the profession to undue influence by the political right. Wealthy individuals (who as a group, and with exceptions, tend to have conservative preferences) establish and endow organizations such as the American Enterprise Institute, the Heritage Foundation and the Media Research Center. These organizations in turn provide the appearance of academic and/or scientific respectability to the viewpoints of their patrons, and act as clearinghouses for reporters seeking sources for the purpose of balancing their reports. Lieberman claims that this gives the news and particularly in-depth discussion of the news, a conservative tilt simply because they make it easier for conservative views to be heard than liberal ones, and make them seem more authoritative by draping them with the mantles of intellectualism and academe.

There can be no doubt that the needs of working journalists, regardless of their personal beliefs, can introduce biases of any or all of several sorts: a preference for a "good" story over a "bad" one; a preference for an adversarial story over a nonadversarial one; or a preference for a story that is fair on the surface over one that is unfair. None of these inherently displays a partisan ideology, but the fact is each could potentially result in partisan consequences in presidential election campaign coverage.

THE BUSINESS OF NEWS

The tension between the need for journalists to practice a profession with high goals and ethical standards and the necessity of a news media outlet to function as a financial entity also has the potential to create biases in news content. For instance, the very notion that an item qualifies as "news" simply because it can attract readers and viewers has already been discussed. The simple truth is that the public at large has no compelling need to know that a certain starlet has a drinking problem or that a given professional athlete has misbehaved in Las Vegas. These items are reported on as news solely because they attract the public's attention to the media outlet, and therefore (in principle) eyeballs to the outlet's advertising.

The dual nature of the news media is explicit in their history. Arthur Gelb (2003) relates the story of Adolph Ochs, then publisher of the *Chattanooga Times*, approaching financier J. P. Morgan for funding to obtain control of *The New York Times*, saying, "I am impelled by only one desire in these negotiations, and that is to secure permanent control of *The New York Times*, which I believe can make a successful and very profitable business enterprise, and at the same time make it the model American newspaper" (p. 4). In short, Ochs regarded profitability as being of a priority equal to journalistic excellence. In 1926 Johnson was making the point that there was a need to attract readers, not only because they support the paper financially, but also because they are necessary to the newspaper being of influence in community affairs. Veteran news anchor Bob Schieffer (2003) makes the same point with regard to CBS's decision to broadcast the release of the Starr report of President Clinton's misbehaviors live: "To be competitive, to be thought of as a serious news organization, we believed we had to go on the air immediately . . . When viewers hear of breaking news and tune to CBS and we are not reporting on it, they switch to another channel and they stay there (p. 359)."

This is of import, of course, because the size of the news hole, that is, the amount of news content that can be transmitted by a single news media outlet such as a newspaper or network news broadcast, is limited in size. This is one of the factors that necessitates the large number of decisions that journalists and editors make. Bagdikian (1971) calculated that some wire service editors were only using about one-fifth of the material they receive on the wire. While the exact proportion of wire service and syndicated material used may have changed since then, the simple facts are that every story put into the news hole of necessity means that another must be excluded to make room for it, and that the process of making these choices leave the people making them open to charges of subjectivity, as was pointed out in chapter 1. It is clearly true that in the days of the Internet and cable TV news, the size of the news hole is much larger in certain places than has been the case in the past, but the simple fact is that it is still not large enough to encompass all the news from everywhere. Someone must make gate-keeping decisions, and the necessity of these decisions means the gatekeepers may be suspected of some form of prejudice or favoritism whenever the news report does not conform to some given user's version of reality.

The impact of the business nature of the news business on the journalistic nature of the news business can be more subtle than simply the idea that news that is economically useful to the business displaces news that might be of import to the reader. Firstly, numerous writers have commented that in bad economic times or for bottom-line reasons it becomes necessary for the news-gathering budget of an outlet to be capped or reduced. Consider *The New York Times*, the *Washington Post*, CBS News and the *Los Angeles Times*—each company's news department has been cut at one or more times since the 1980s—and in fact the *Los Angeles Times* and the *Washington Post* went through another round of cutbacks in summer 2008. Our local Hartford *Courant* has cut news staff from 400 in 1994 to 135 in 2009, and was in the process of cutting again in 2011 (Gosselin, 2011). This is presumed to lead to a reduction in the quality of the news operations, and also to an increased homogeneity of content between outlets as they rely more heavily on relatively inexpensive syndicated content and/or share resources. This, of course, can include coverage of presidential election campaigns.

This is a particular problem in the field of network television, in which the entertainment division and the news division are sometimes in conflict, competing for time in the limited broadcast schedule. Prime-time news hours were not uncommon in the 1950s, exemplified by shows such as Edward R. Murrow's *See It Now*. By the 1970s, however, this was considered no longer commercially viable. Veteran reporter Bill Moyers specifically pitched the idea of a prime-time news show to CBS chairman Bill Paley as part of his terms for staying with CBS, only to be told, "I'm sorry, Bill. I can't do it any more. The minute is worth too much now" (Halberstam, 1979, p. 734). Similarly, events such as the Nixon concession speech that set the stage for this book are no longer broadcast live on network newscasts; instead, they would be handled as a news item of a minute or less consisting of a news brief and a short sound bite. (It should be noted that in the current media environment, Nixon's press conference would probably have been aired in its entirety by cable news channels such as CNN, particularly if they had known in advance of its extraordinary content, but, as noted, Nixon had not been expected to speak and the content of his speech was previously unknown.)

Secondly, as news media outlets are managed as businesses meant to maximize profits to the exclusion of their journalistic goals, they sometimes adopt practices that are potentially or actually harmful to the reporting of news. For instance, in the late 1980s, cable TV mogul Ted Turner had decided to make a corporate takeover of CBS. To prevent this from happening, the CBS corporate board of directors authorized a large buyback of CBS's stock, which had the short-term effects of simultaneously driving the stock price up (making the takeover more expensive) and making CBS an unattractive takeover target by incurring a large corporate debt that Turner would have to pay back. Turner backed down in his bid; unfortunately, this left CBS to pay off the debt incurred, leading to across-the-board budget cuts, including to the news division (Schieffer, 2003).

There are similar examples from other outlets. For instance, the stock market crash of 1987 led eventually to a loss of about 40 percent of ad linage from *The New York Times*. At that time the news department was ordered to find $1,000,000 in savings, leading to a reduction in the number of syndicated columns being printed and buyouts of contracts from reporters. Similarly, the *Times* was revamped somewhat in the mid-1980s to become more "user-friendly," including the addition of news analysis and soft-news features on page one for the first time, along with color photography and a six-column format. This move was made in part to improve the *Times'* competitive position vis-a-vis *USA Today* and the *Wall Street Journal*, despite the fact that it was a departure from the *Times'* practice of presenting factually based news stories on page one (Gelb, 2003).

The notion of a news industry as a business is likely to have several types of impact on the content of the news. For instance, Page and Shapiro (1992) have pointed out that in the United States the news can have both pro-capitalist and minimal government biases, both positions consistent with the existence of a news medium that is constructed as a for-profit entity in a capitalist society. Any other position would be antithetical to the successful future existence of the business; while individual news media outlets might express preference for governmental regulation of their industries, on the whole it would not be in their best interests.

Ideologically, it is important to recall that the way media industries make money is by attracting users who pay subscription fees, read advertising, take out classified ads, and so forth. It is also useful to recall that political attitudes throughout the nation are distributed more or less normally, and so therefore there are larger audiences at the center of the political spectrum than there are at the extremes.

Economic analyses have demonstrated that, in a multi-channel environment such as that represented by the cable TV industry or the magazine publishing business, channels and outlets appealing to either end of the political spectrum can attract niche audiences and succeed economically (e.g., Xiang & Sarvary, 2007). This is the essence of the notion of "narrowcasting" and has been successful not only for political niche audiences but also in reaching a wide variety of demographic and psychographics groupings. This analysis is probably at the basis of the founding of the Fox News Channel, with its deliberate attempt to program and appeal to the political right, and Air America Radio and its programming for politically liberal audiences.

In media markets containing a small number of outlets, however, the most desirable political ground is the center. Consequently, this is the political position many local print outlets, specifically newspapers, should be expected to take for business reasons. It has been noted repeatedly that the number of communities in which there are competing print outlets is declining as newspapers either go bankrupt and shut down, or consolidate into jointly operating entities (c.f. Straubhaar & LaRose, 2006). The process by which this happens is fairly well-known: consider a market able to support two newspapers in good economic times. When there is an economic downturn, however, the amount of money local businesses have available for purchase of advertising tends to decline. In those times advertising tends to go to the paper with the larger subscriber base, whichever paper it is and whatever its ideology. (Obviously there are advertising purchases that are ideologically driven, but for the most part retailers simply want the most possible return for their advertising, a desire that is magnified in bad times.) Neiva (1996) points out, for instance, that post–World War II changes in technology and labor relations caused the proportion of single newspaper markets to increase to 90 percent by 1948. Publishers (and publishing families) unprepared to deal with the changing business environment, and the rise in the importance of a newspaper's business nature, were driven out of their markets, leaving the field to business-oriented persons. Compaine (1980) shows that this trend continued into the 1970s, by which time 98 percent of newspaper markets were served by only one local paper. Schulhofer-Wohl and Garrido (2009) claim that only eleven U.S. cities had competing daily newspapers in 2009, down from 15 in 2008 and 689 in 1910.

This winnowing process strongly suggests that surviving papers were those best able to deal with the business aspect of the news media, as the inability to do so made many newspapers financially impossible to operate. Thus, since the ideological center is where the largest audience is, it is arguably a survival trait for the newspaper to locate itself toward the political center, appealing to the largest audience and offending the least number of people. Klapper (1961) has pointed this out in his discussion of why media tend to reinforce existing attitudes rather than changing them wholesale.

It must be noted, however, that when we are discussing local media, we have to take into account that not all communities are the same politically. While a national medium such as CBS can and should appeal to the political center of the nation to achieve maximal exposure to users, a local newspaper should ideally appeal to the political center of the community it serves, and there is some evidence (Kang, 2007) that this is the case. Measured against the absolute standard of the nation's center, papers serving communities that were substantially more conservative or liberal than the nation as a whole and whose coverage reflected the local politics would appear to have ideological biases. These biases, however, would better be described as economic rather than ideological, an attempt to maximize audience share by catering to the audience's preferences.

And, as should be clear from the discussion above, a multi-channel or competitive media environment should increase the likelihood that one or more of those outlets would deliberately select an ideologically biased position as a competitive commercial decision, or could make an ideologically driven decision to adopt a biased position that would nonetheless succeed economically. The multi-channel environment allows the delivery of specialized audiences to advertisers willing to pay premium prices for access to them, and one way of developing specialized audiences is to distinguish them on the left-right political spectrum. So while the economics of noncompetitive environments should tend to drive news content to the local ideological center, this effect is moderated in competitive environments. Specifically, a new news media outlet entering a market or competing in a market against a competitor with a larger market share and a moderate/centrist ideology would be encouraged economically to present a product with a distinct ideological bias. That said, on the whole there is no economic preference for liberal or conservative ideology and thus, on the whole, in terms of "the media" as an aggregate, there should be no overall effect.

The dependence of most traditional news media outlets (TV and radio stations, newspapers) on advertising places an element of economic control into the hands of advertisers. Later in this chapter the action of several advertisers in preventing the airing of a controversial documentary will be discussed, and

Reuter and Zitzewitz (2006) suggest there is a modicum of control of news by advertisers, at least in the business pages. Sutter (2002) demonstrates the inefficiencies of this, though: if advertisers force news media outlets to adopt positions uncongenial to the users, users are alienated from the outlet and in turn its advertising. The data suggests that advertisers can have ideological impacts but for the most part, with the exception of very specific issues or events, they do not.

News Media Outlets as Property

Although a given news media outlet is both a journalistic entity needing to achieve the goals of its profession and a business needing to attract sufficient revenue to maintain its existence, it is important to recognize that both of these natures are moderated by the fact that in a capitalistic society, the outlet is also the property of some person or corporate entity. As will be seen, the type of control can be dependent on the nature of the ownership—private owners, for instance, arguably have more options open to them than corporate officers who are responsible to their shareholders—but within the limits imposed by the laws governing financial activity, owners can do much as they please.

This is possible, of course, because the news businesses, like most American businesses, are largely hierarchical in structure, with some combination of owner, president, CEO, publisher and/or board of directors at the top of the hierarchy. This puts those people, as Liebling (1961/1975) has pointed out, in a position of means control over the actions of all subordinate employees. As Rivers (1965) puts it, quoting an old poet, "Whose wine I drink, his song I play." This is considered of import because, as shown previously, in the same way that there is a generalized tendency for news reporters to be liberal and therefore expected to influence news toward the left, there is a generalized tendency for business owners to be conservative. Thus, they are expected to use their power in the organizational hierarchy to influence news toward the right.

There is substantial anecdotal evidence that owners and publishers can make use of their organizational position at the top of the hierarchy to influence the nature of news coverage; for instance, consider the *Los Angeles Times* outlined in chapter 1. In its early days the Otis and Chandler families created a specific policy of creating a good business climate in the then-developing state of California. This orientation included opposition to taxation and labor movements, and a general promotion of the area and Republican party candidates as being allies with the *Times* in promoting economic growth and fighting unions (Halberstam, 1979). This policy can clearly be seen, for instance, in content analyses of the *Times'* coverage of the 1952 and 1960 presidential campaigns (Blumberg, 1954; Stempel, 1961). In each case, the *Times'* coverage of Republican candidates swamped that of their Democratic opponents. The accession of Otis Chandler to the publisher's chair of the *Los Angeles Times* led to, among other consequences, the decision to lead the paper's news content toward political moderation; in fact this change is part of the subtext of Nixon's reaction to his 1962 coverage. (Halberstam reports that Chandler drove this change in ideology as a result of desire to improve the national reputation of the newspaper.)

Numerous other examples abound. *Time* magazine during the reign of Henry Luce is cited repeatedly as an example of a news outlet whose coverage is written and/or edited to conform to the prejudices of the publisher; in fact, Liebling's classic *The Press* (1961/1975) contains a section titled "The Rubber-Type Army" that attempts to dig through *Time*'s propaganda about the Nationalist Chinese Army. (Luce, who had lived in China with his missionary parents, was a friend of then-Nationalist Chinese leader Chiang Kai-shek and used *Time* to advance Chiang's causes at every opportunity.) Veteran reporter Bob Schieffer (2003) started his career with the *Fort Worth Star Telegram*, founded and published by the multimillionaire Amon Carter to promote Fort Worth and West Texas, with actual news values being secondary to his social agenda. Reverend Sun Myung Moon and his Unification church founded and publish the *Washington Times* specifically to advance the conservative beliefs of himself and his church (United Press International, 1982). More recently, *Editor and Publisher* reported orders on the part of Richard Mellon Scaife, owner and publisher of the *Pittsburgh Tribune-Review*, to "bury" Al Gore's 2000 presidential campaign (Lieberman, 2000).

That owners and publishers use means control to influence the content of news outlets by controlling employees also appears to be the case. Leo Rosten's 1937 poll of the Washington press corps discovered that over half had had stories cut or killed for ideological reasons and three in five knew that they were expected to slant their stories in specific ways. Rivers (1965) claims that these figures had fallen to 7 percent and under 10 percent by the early 1960s, although he also cites Eugene Pulliam, then head of Central Newspapers and owner of the *Indianapolis Star*, *Arizona Republic* and several other newspapers and radio stations, as a contemporary (mid-1960s) example of a publisher wanting the news told his way. Even as late as 2004 two editors of the *Jupiter* (FL) *Courier* resigned rather than yield to instructions from corporate owner Scripps-Howard on campaign coverage (Rosen, 2004). In broader terms, Bagdikian (1972), Kahn and Kenney (2002) and D'Alessio and Allen (2006) all found associations between editorial endorsements (typically made by, or with input from, publishers) and news coverage of political candidates. Endorsed candidates generally got better news cover-age, in as many as 81 of 84 cases in Bagdikian's report (associations were not that strong but still substantial in the other two studies).

The question of what sort of influence ownership exerts over news content is made substantially more complex by the myriad types of media owner-ship. Altschull (1984) identifies four major models or exemplars of media ownership. The first is an "official" model in which the news media outlets are state-owned or controlled. An example of this in the United States is the Government Printing Office, one of the largest publishers in the nation. Second, there are interest groups that fund media to further their organiza-tional interests. For example, the widest-circulating magazine in the United States is *AARP, the Magazine*, which not only communicates to members of the American Association of Retired Persons but also attempts to mobilize and channelize the political voices of senior citizens. Third, there are media whose ownership is "informal" but represents the views of contributors, such as a blog or Internet newsgroup might. The fourth type, commercial media, are presumed to represent the interests of owners and advertisers. Obviously, each of these ownership models is expected to create pressures to bend news content to their own ends, which is Altschull's point in identifying them.

Even with the most common model in place in the United States, at least among those news media outlets supplying formal news coverage of politi-cal campaigns, the commercial model, there are wide and potentially influ-ential differences between the ownership structures of some news media outlets and others. In broad terms, news outlets are either owned publicly, that is, by offering ownership shares in the company publicly on major stock markets such as the New York Stock Exchange, or privately, in which the shares are distributed among a smaller, and closed, group of investors. As examples, ABC television (and thus ABC network news) is owned by the Walt Disney Company, a publicly owned corporation whose shares are listed on the NYSE; contrariwise, the Tribune Company, publisher of the *Los Angeles Times*, *Chicago Tribune*, *Baltimore Sun* and ten other newspapers, as well as television and radio stations, is currently privately owned by a consortium headed by Sam Zell, who bought out public shareholders in 2007 (Ahrens, 2007).

But even within these broad categories there are other distinctions as well. *The New York Times*, for instance, distributes Class A shares of The New York Times Corporation via the NYSE; however, the Board of Directors of the corporation is largely (70 percent) controlled by holders of the Class B shares, which are retained solely by the Ochs/Sulzberger family. The family recently declined requests by Class A shareholders to make control of the corporation public (Thomas, 2007). Another complex ownership structure is that of the *Milwaukee Journal-Sentinel*, which is technically a privately owned company. The *Journal-Sentinel* is actually cooperatively controlled by its employees, the public and the family of former chairman Harry Grant. However, employees control 86 percent of the votes on management issues the public 12 percent and the Grant family 2 percent (Journal Communications, 2007). Employees cannot sell or give away their shares; they must give them up when they leave the company.

Both public and private media companies can also be classified by whether they are essentially stand-alone outlets that operate independently of other outlets, even those owned by the same company, or part of a chain that shares some elements of editorial and news content.

It is sometimes presumed that a chain of papers, particularly a privately owned chain, will all speak with one voice. In *Voting*, for instance, Berelson, Lazarsfeld and McPhee (1954), refer to the chain-owned Elmira newspapers: " . . . The Republican press in a Republican town in what was for the American press generally a 'Republican year.' Elmira's three newspapers, all published by Frank Gannett, were Republican, and they showed it" (p. 239). Chain ownership is presupposed to lead to a decrease in the number of editorial voices as the chain owner is presumed to dictate editorial choices for all papers in the chain. As it happens, the sheer corporate mass of a chain and the disparate needs of individual outlets in the chain can mitigate this control. For instance, Busterna and Hansen (1990) showed that chain ownership ended up having a fairly small impact on editorial endorsements in presidential campaigns in the 1970s and 1980s.

The private versus public nature of the ownership of the outlet can have important implications in terms of the political content and bias of its news content under specific circumstances. It is expected, for instance, that publicly owned companies are managed in such a way as to provide their shareholders with a return on their investments. This brings the nature of the outlet as a business to the fore, and can reasonably lead to the sorts of biases favoring centrist positions and local community values, as we saw when we considered the business nature of a news media outlet previously. An example of this occurred in the 2004 campaign when publicly owned Sinclair Broadcast Group scheduled the anti–John Kerry documentary *Stolen Honor* for airing. Advertisers including Burger King and Staples pulled ads from Sinclair's TV stations (Rubin, 2004), causing the company's stock to decline in value and in turn leading to a shareholder lawsuit, which was subsequently dropped (Associate Press Financial Wire, 2005). The documentary was pulled from the broadcast schedule before airing.

Privately owned outlets can put their political views ahead of the cause of profit to the extent that they can afford to and are willing to. In a memorable sequence of his masterpiece *Citizen Kane*, Orson Welles as Charles Foster Kane famously declares what the guiding principles of his newspaper will be. Carter, the stodgy old editor, declares that the newspaper is not interested in the story of a woman who is missing, rumored to be murdered. "Mr. Carter," Kane replies, "That's the kind of thing we are going to be interested in from now on" (Welles, 1941). He can do this because he is the owner of the paper; it is his property, and he can do with it as he pleases. Although fictional, the scene nonetheless possesses verisimilitude. A privately owned news media outlet is the owner's property and, within the legal restrictions imposed on privately owned businesses, generally is his or hers to do with as he or she wills. There is no legal or moral requirement that the owner make money; only that the outlet meet its financial obligations. In the absence of the necessity of placating the public in order to give shareholders a return on investment, it is not unreasonable to presume that the news coverage provided by a privately owned outlet will take the tone best suited to the needs, wants and desires of the owner.

A Political Press

The fourth nature of the news media industry relevant to this discussion is its role as the so-called "fourth estate of government." While the term was not meant for the United States (legend has it that Edmund Burke coined the phrase to apply to the nineteenth-century English press), there is still the tendency to see the press as operating both cooperatively and competitively with the executive, legislative and judicial branches to enable the processes of representative democracy to function properly.

This is itself a complex social function driven by a myriad of social, political and regulatory forces. Whereas the owner of a newspaper may make a conscious decision to do as he or she pleases (when we consider a news media outlet as property), as a player in the political game the news media outlet is both an actor and an object to be acted upon, with substantially less individual freedom.

The power of news media outlets in the political process lies in their ability to convey information to the public. In some cases this is information that a given governmental branch wishes to have conveyed. There are many times when for its own purposes a governmental entity must make certain pieces of information—a political situation report, or knowledge of the passage of a new law, for instance—known to the electorate, and the easiest conduit for that information to the people is the news media. At the same time, there is information that a government official or unit might not desire to have known, such as knowledge of an official's questionable business dealings. The power of the press in the political process lies in its control of that conduit of information between government and electorate.

This is sometimes the explicit reason for the existence or justification for the existence of a specific outlet. The Graham family, for instance, was adamant about obtaining control of the *Washington Post* in the 1950s explicitly for the purpose of having the access to the political processes of Washington that a newspaper in the city would provide (Halberstam, 1979). Similarly, virtually all major newspapers have routinely established bureaus in the capitals of their respective states (if the newspaper is not already located in the capital).

At the same time, the news media have two weaknesses as a political player. First, economically, as we have seen, they exist to deliver users to advertisers, and the mechanism by which they do this is by providing news of interest to their users. It is a popular media image to envision the news media as having insatiable appetites for content, but at the base of this image is a simple truth: there has to be enough news to fill the news hole every single day, no more, no less. So if government officials are dependent on news outlets for the communication of information to the electorate, so, too, are news media outlets dependent to a degree on government sources. In the case discussed above, for instance, following the heated debate surrounding the decision of Sinclair Broadcasting to air *Stolen Honor* and subsequent cancellation of the program described earlier, Sinclair's Washington bureau chief resigned, claiming that that the pervasive right-wing bias in Sinclair's news reporting had made it impossible for him to do his job. "No Democrats would talk to me," he told *Broadcasting & Cable* magazine. "They would schedule interviews and then cancel them—fast—as soon as they did their homework. Who could blame them?" (PR Newswire, 2004).

This interdependence of reporter and politician has lead to the evolution of an elaborate dance between sources and reporters that seems almost insane in its complexity. Information may be provided "on the record," "off the record" or as "background." Sources of information can sometimes be cited by name, or as "official sources" or "government sources" or even as "anonymous sources" depending on the nature of the information (on or off the record). Because of the interdependence between sources and outlets, this elaborate charade is played out routinely. In fact, reporters have complained that some officials (particularly in the Carter administration) did not understand the system and would become upset when they were quoted, despite their desire not to be, when they described the information they were providing using the wrong classificatory term (Schieffer, 2003).

It has been argued that this creates an "us versus them" mentality, not between sources and reporters but between the political actors (sources and political reporters) and outsiders. The political actors perceive themselves to be in a cooperative position, the argument goes, and come to an accommodation that is mutually beneficial. At election time, this is expected to lead to an advantage for the incumbent, presuming that the incumbent has not made active enemies of the press corps, for two reasons: first, because the press is believed to have a preference for the people with whom they have already negotiated a successful working relationship, and second, because the successful working relationship between incumbent and press corps should make it easier for the incumbent to communicate critical campaign information through the news media to the electorate. This is called a pro-incumbency bias, and there is some evidence of its existence. Graber (1976) uncovered patterns of newspaper coverage consistent with a pro-incumbent bias in coverage of the 1972 campaign. (Ironically, the incumbent benefiting was none other than Richard Nixon!) Prior (2006) also suggests that pro-incumbency biases in local TV news coverage are partly responsible for the high reelection rates of representatives, particularly among less well-educated voters.

News media outlets also have a political identity that is essentially legal in nature. Newspapers, and in practice newsmagazines, have the specific protections provided by the First Amendment to the Constitution. These protections are broad and powerful, and can only be circumvented in the direst of circumstances, such as in the face of a "clear and present danger" to the nation or where such circumvention leads to prevention of an even larger abuse of other constitutional rights (Wagman, 1991).

This is not completely the case for the broadcast media, which of course include the network news programming provided daily to virtually every household in America. Broadcast media are considered legitimate subject for certain forms of restriction because they use a scarce resource, the electromagnetic broadcast spectrum that is legally the property of the people of the United States and administered in their name by the government (Wagman, 1991).

The concentration of communication power into the hands of commercial entities who were nonetheless charged with operating those channels in the best interest of the public that owned them led to regulatory restrictions meant to assist the stations in meeting that charge. Two of them were the Fairness Doctrine and the Equal Time Provision. TV and radio news was charged by the Federal Communications Commission, under penalty of fine, suspension or loss of license, with treating issues and candidates fairly and to provide equal time for people speaking on either side of a given issue. In practice, rather than give away time that could be filled with advertisements, stations tended not to take positions on issues or candidates, which is to say they tended to take a centrist or even apolitical positions.

The Fairness Doctrine and Equal Time Provision were relaxed in the early 1980s. It was Reagan administration policy that marketplace forces would work to have the intended effect of those regulations, which was to showcase viewpoints consistent with significant numbers of audience members. However, reimposition by legislative fiat has been threatened by congressional leaders periodically ever since, although the Fairness Doctrine was ultimately declared unconstitutional (Straubhaar & LaRose, 2006). The upshot of this, however, is a broad tendency for the network TV news to avoid controversy in part by generally reducing the amount of political coverage offered to the public, although this trend reversed somewhat for the 2004 presidential campaign (Farnsworth & Lichter, 2007).

It must be noted that this is not necessarily the case in the cable TV industry. Cable news stations such as CNN and Fox News are operating in an environment of now hundreds of channels meeting all sorts of specialized needs, including several (CSPAN 1, 2 and 3) that specialize in real-time coverage of politics and candidates. In addition, cable TV is a separate realm in terms of legal restrictions, which are much looser for cable TV than broadcast TV because cable providers use their own distribution systems, not the public airwaves. As discussed above, CNN and Fox News are in a position to attempt to serve ideologically based niche audiences, and in fact one of the criticisms of Fox News is that it serves a conservative agenda even as it claims to be fair and balanced. But broadcast network TV news reports face strong pressure, from a tradition of apoliticism backed by possible re-regulation as well as the economic need to seek a large audience, to stick close to the ideological center in their content.

This discussion clearly implies that the different regulatory situations of broadcast outlets versus print and cable allow the latter greater flexibility in adopting ideologically biased positions. All news media outlets have the need to get and transmit news and so the pro-incumbency bias, if there is one, should be pervasive. It should also be nonpartisan, however, based on mechanical processes and mutual advantage, not rooted in an ideological basis.

On the other hand, the freer regulatory structure of the print and cable industries allows them greater latitude to respond to the other forces acting on them. It also provides increased flexibility with which to respond to the needs of journalists and journalism, the needs of economics and sales, and the needs of owners and ownership.

The Complex Forces on News

To summarize the key points, it needs to be made clear that news media outlets are not simple entities but instead part of a complex socioeconomic matrix, creating not a single force to influence news reporting in one direction, but numerous forces creating an intricate vortex of biases. Four we can identify immediately are:

* Media are economic entities that function to make money. To fail to do so is to fail the shareholders, public or private, in their investment;
* Media are political actors that function as a conduit between political actors and the populace, and that fulfill an oversight function on political processes. To fail to do so is to fail the electorate;
* Media are property that function to work the will of the owner. To fail to do so is to deprive the owner of his or her property rights; and
* Media are journalistic entities within the confines of which professional persons pursue their craft. To fail to do so is to reject the professional needs of the employees.

This discussion should make it clear that expectations such as "reporters are liberal, therefore the media are liberal" or "owners are conservative, therefore the media are conservative" are overly simplistic and fail to account for the economic, political, and professional factors that potentially act to introduce their own biases in news media content. Unfortunately, there have been very few attempts to reconcile the impacts of economic, professional, legislative and personal forces on a news media outlet's news content. Donohew (1967) did attempt to contrast the impact of a publisher's opinion with those of the economic forces created by the local audience's opinions to see which showed the greatest impact on bias. He found essentially that the community's views has no effect while the owner's views were associated with congruent biases; but one would expect the owner's voice to speak more loudly in the short run. Ownership can be revolutionary but economics must be evolutionary.

In fact, when considering all of the perspectives on the nature of media industries as journalistic, economic, and political entities as well as the property of owners who are sometimes private actors but also sometimes publicly owned corporations, it would seem the most likely expectation that the news reports in the news media tend to be strongly centrist in orientation. A point from chapter 1 needs to be reiterated at this point as a caveat, of course: that this discussion pertains specifically and solely to the news content of the news media. Commentary, opinion and editorial material are the intellectual property of the creator and may express whatever viewpoints the creator chooses. But news reporting on the whole should reasonably be expected to be ideologically neutral. The media (as a group) should be expected to be neither liberal nor conservative; the structure of the news media industry in the

United States and the forces acting on news media outlets should lead to the expectation that news coverage would be moderate, or centrist, in ideology.

That said, although that may be the case for the media industries as a whole, it is certainly within the realm of possibility, and in fact to be expected, that individual news outlets can and will be willing to sacrifice professional integrity or maximum potential economic gain for the purpose of advocating an ideological goal. A publicly owned outlet is answerable to the shareholders; a privately owned outlet answerable only to the conscience (and pocketbook) of the owners. If Richard Mellon Scaife wants to order his paper to bury the Gore campaign, he can: it's his paper. That can swing the *Pittsburgh Tribune-Review*'s content to the right of the ideological center, and in consequence that particular outlet's coverage can be fairly described as biased. But such a decision is arguably also offensive to readers who are left of center, and opens room in the Pittsburgh market for a competitor with a left-of-center viewpoint. And so two biased outlets potentially lead to a media structure that is balanced, more or less, in the aggregate.

It is also important to recognize that, given information on coverage patterns by media outlets, it should be possible to consider the impact of at least some of the structural elements discussed earlier in this chapter on the content of news outlets. It is expected, from the discussion above, that publicly owned outlets should be more closely aligned with the political middle than privately owned outlets. With information on the degree of balance in coverage and the nature of ownership, that expectation becomes empirically testable, and in fact it will be tested (in chapter 5).

Similarly, if it is possible to determine the ideology of the owners of specific outlets (and the ideology of owners of newspapers, at least, is often accessible through the editorial positions taken by their papers), then it should be possible to determine whether there is an association, presumably causal (via the mechanism of owners possessing means-control over staffers), between the owner's ideology and bias, if any, in the news outlet's news coverage. It is as much of an oversimplification to claim that because owners tend to be wealthy and the wealthy tend to be conservative, therefore all owners are conservative as it is to claim that reporters as a group tend to be liberal, therefore all reporters are liberal. In fact there is a long tradition of liberalism among a number of wealthy families, notable examples including the Kennedys, the Roosevelts, the Grahams, and the Ochs and the Sulzbergers. The ability of an owner to influence news content in accord with his or her ideology, regardless of valence, should be measurable.

Another specific question that can potentially be answered is the degree to which the media's charge to be a watchdog over political processes influences their coverage of candidates and campaigns varies depending on whether the candidate is an incumbent or challenging an incumbent. Not all presidential elections involve incumbent candidates, but it should be clear that a sitting president has different opportunities to influence news and its coverage than a challenger, and also has a different relationship with the press than a challenger. Will this manifest itself in differences in coverage between incumbents and challengers? This, too, should be subject to analysis and test.

The purpose of these analyses is ultimately to answer key questions about the existence and magnitude of partisan bias in news coverage of presidential election campaigns, and more importantly, to examine elements of the media industries and the economic, political and regulatory circumstances that have the potential to influence partisan bias, either by ameliorating or exacerbating it. The methodology employed to examine these questions is the subject of chapter 3.

3

The Challenges of Measuring Bias

It is not useful to conduct any formal study of the sources and magnitudes of media bias without first acknowledging two things. First, it must be accepted that media news reports contain a wide variety of information, including some news media outlet somewhere, that is supportive of almost any ideological viewpoint. Media people, including reporters, editors, publishers and owners, are too different individually for anything else to be true. It is established that reporters tend to have liberal personal politics and owners conservative, but there are also conservative reporters and liberal owners, regardless of the general ideological tendencies of the groups. The problem with media bias, to the extent that there is one, therefore, is not that viewpoints are not represented but rather that there is favoritism in the presentation: one side gets more coverage, or better coverage, than the other. Second, we must be aware that the perception of media bias is a subjective process. That is, whether or not a given observer thinks that something that appears in a given news report or series of news reports is biased depends in part on the personal ideology of the observer.

The multiplicity of viewpoints presented in the media leaves them open to charges of bias based on the use of a reasoning process called "confirmation bias" or "instance confirmation" (c.f. Musgrave, 1974). Basically, when leveling a charge of media bias, it is almost always possible to find specific instances of elements—stories, paragraphs, photographs, video—that confirm one's charge, regardless of the nature and valence of the bias being imputed, simply because those elements are present somewhere in the giant corpus of content that is the media. In fact, it is instance confirmation that Richard Nixon indulged himself in when he pointed out that a mistake he had made was reported and his opponent's mistake was not (see chapter 1). Wanting to

believe that the media were against him, he picked out an instance of reporting that was unfavorable to himself, ignoring any situations where he might
have received the benefit over his opponent, and offered that single instance
as "proof" of bias against him.

In formal scientific terms, the problem with instance confirmation as a
method of making knowledge claims is that it relies on an unrepresentative
cross-section of media content. It should be obvious that if an observer is al-
lowed to select from an entire body of work any examples of instances that
support his or her point and ignore any that do not, said observer should be
readily able to amass a substantial set of examples and present a large number
of cases, making his or her argument appear quite persuasive. Yet the conclusion reached by this process could quite possibly be entirely incorrect.

Unfortunately, this is exactly the sort of reasoning used by many critics of
the media on either side of the ideological spectrum. It is not uncommon for
a commentator to hold up an article, often of which only the headline (which
is typically not written by the reporter but by an editor) or a photograph is
intelligible and claim, "Is this not an example of biased reporting?" The conclusion the user is invited to reach is agreement, although, as we are aware
from chapter 1, the correct answer is "No," as bias is by definition systematic
and sustained and not a function of a single instance of reporting. While a
single article can be unbalanced or unfair for any one of a number of reasons
including, but not limited to, actual malice on the part of the reporter, the editor, the publisher or the entire news media outlet, coverage is biased only if it
is unbalanced in a sustained way, not in a single instance.

A related tactic is to make a broad charge of bias and offer no specific evidence at all. This has happened repeatedly across a number of campaigns and
issues, and is effective because instances supporting any viewpoint can be
found if they are looked for hard enough. By making unsubstantiated claims,
the critic invites users to seek out their own examples and, for all intents and
purposes, persuade themselves of the "truth" of the critic's point. As it happens, the time pressures of news reporting often preclude the formal examination of an entire body of content as the debate on an issue runs; not many
news media outlets have the resources or motivation to assign two editors to
oversee their reporting as the *Los Angeles Times* did in 1962 (Halberstam,
1979). So the charge is leveled and users subsequently locate instances of reporting that confirm—incorrectly or inadequately—the charge well founded,
thus "proving" the truth of the charge.

In order to prevent the transmission of false information resulting from
the use of instance confirmation, it is necessary to either examine an entire
body of coverage or a randomly selected subset of it. The taking of samples
from a known population is a technique commonly practiced by pollsters and

social scientists; characteristics of the population can be inferred from the sample while reducing the amount of material to be analyzed to a manageable amount (c.f. Babbie, 2001; Wimmer & Dominick, 2011).

If we stop to consider solely the coverage of a campaign for the presidency of the United States, for example, the amount of material is already arguably manageable in amount. For instance, I personally examined all the photographs published on the front page of *The New York Times* for every issue from Labor Day to Election Day of 1948, and can say with absolute confidence that there were exactly five photographs of presidential candidates that appeared on the front pages of *The New York Times* during the traditional campaign period. That four of them were of President Truman and only one of his opponent, Governor Dewey, may or may not be evidence of anything. What is important is that it is a manageable amount of content to deal with, and it is also the sum total of all the front-page photographs of presidential candidates appearing on the front pages of the issues of *The New York Times* during the 1948 campaign; that is, it is the population of all *Times* front-page photos of presidential candidates.

Access to the population of all content elements, whether they are photographs, stories, lines of text, quotations or whatever, implies that proper procedure is to deal with them as a whole. It is poor reasoning to point at the single picture of Governor Dewey and from that infer a bias against President Truman. Rather, one concludes that 80 percent of the photographs printed on the front page of *The New York Times* during the 1948 campaign were of President Truman, and draws whatever conclusions may be appropriate from the whole rather than instances deliberately or accidentally selected from the whole.

SUBJECTIVITY OF BIAS JUDGMENTS

Interpretation of the meaning of content elements, even if they come from a valid sample or population, must be done carefully. As a point of demonstrable fact, the tendency is for a person who holds one position on an issue to look at a news report and to judge it to be biased against that position even as a person of a opposing position on the same issue looks at the same news report and claims that it is also biased against the opposing position. This is known as the "hostile media effect," that is, the tendency to see the media as hostile to your ideology regardless of either the nature of your ideology or the actual content of the news media report in question (c.f. Vallone, Ross & Lepper, 1985; Giner-Sorolla & Chaiken, 1994; Gunther & Schmitt, 2004).

The hostile media effect is one example of a well-known phenomenon called selective perception, which is the tendency of people to interpret (or misinterpret) the meaning of observations in terms of their preexisting beliefs and attitudes. Hastorf and Cantril (1954) observed a classic example of selective perception when they talked to members of the crowd at a Dartmouth/ Princeton football game in 1951. That year Princeton had been favored but lost the game, during which their biggest star had been injured. After the game Dartmouth fans described the game as "rough but fair" while Princeton rooters called it "unfair and dirty"—despite the fact that they had all seen exactly the same game. The only difference between the two groups lay in their preexisting attitudes, and thus it is clear that their attitudes had influenced their interpretation of what they had seen.

In studies of the hostile media effect a typical research design calls for groups of people on either side of an issue they feel strongly about—for instance, Arab-Israeli relations (Vallone, Ross & Lepper, 1985), presidential campaigns (Dalton, Beck and Huckfeldt, 1998) or ethical issues (Gunther & Christen, 2002)—to be shown a news report on the issue. The hostile media effect implies that each side will see the report as biased against them even when the stimulus story is in fact fair and balanced, or even already favorable to their side. (In fact, D'Alessio [2003] has shown that readers frequently identify the quotations from their opponents as being examples of media bias, even though the quotations are the only part of the story not in the words of the reporter!)

The hostile media effect has also been demonstrated in a field study of presidential campaign coverage. Culbertson and Stempel (1991) asked readers of the *Louisville Courier-Journal* and the *Chicago Tribune* whether their paper was biased in its reporting. Respondents who intended to vote against the candidate endorsed by their paper (Mondale for the *Courier-Journal* and Reagan for the *Tribune*) were almost twice as likely to say the paper's coverage was biased than respondents intending to vote for the endorsed candidate (47 percent to 25 percent). Yet each group of people had been exposed on a daily basis to the same coverage, at least within their respective municipalities. Again it is seen that people see bias in certain material depending on their own beliefs.

It is therefore unreasonable to conclude that specific news reports and the media generally are biased simply because people claim that they are. Further, being people themselves, politicians, political commentators and media critics are as subject to the hostile media effect as any other person.

Another means of examining the subjective nature of media bias would be to compare beliefs about bias with actual news content. Using computer-based textual analysis techniques coupled with the results of a number of public opinion polls conducted across a lengthy period of time, Watts, Domke, Shah and Fan (1999) showed that the public's perception of the magnitude of bias in the media was more closely associated with charges made through the media that the media were biased than the actual content of the media themselves. In short, what seems to happen is that when charges of media bias are leveled, peoples' beliefs that the media are biased are reinforced, even though the content itself remains approximately the same. This combination of laboratory and field study results is strong evidence that the perception of media bias is subjective in nature.

Potential explanations for the hostile media effect lies in a combination of the requirements of ethical news reporting with basic human nature. As we have already seen, the professional expectations of news reporting are that news reports are to be fair and balanced. That is, that in a given news report, opposing viewpoints on an issue are to be represented and presented with roughly equal respect, regardless of the personal opinion of the reporter (see chapter 2). This means, of necessity, that an article on an issue of import to a given observer will contain elements that the observer agrees with and elements the observer disagrees with, as they are presented together in order for the reporter to be fair to both sides.

If the news report is considered theoretically as a persuasive message, reasons for the user's perception that it is hostile becomes clear. The elements of the story that the reader agrees with are simply accepted by the user as being true uncritically, as the user already believes them to be true. The elements the user disagrees with, however, can be aversively stimulating, which is to say that the consumers are motivated to counteract them in some way. In balance-oriented models of cognition such as dissonance theory (Festinger, 1957), for instance, story elements the user disagrees with generate dissonant feelings that the user is motivated to counteract by denigrating the source (i.e., calling it "biased"). Although theories related to the concept of cognitive balance are currently out of vogue, there is recent evidence that they have been rejected prematurely (D'Alessio & Allen, 2002). Schmitt, Gunther and Liebhart (2004) attribute the hostile media effect to a phenomenon they call selective categorization, in which partisans on an issue interpret the same information differently from partisans with different opinions depending on their perspectives—exactly as Hastorf and Cantril (1954) observed.

Similarly, theoretical models of persuasion based on the idea of users responding cognitively to persuasive elements (c.f. Petty, Ostrom & Brock, 1981) would predict that story elements that receivers agree with would be accepted uncritically but those they disagree with would generate negative cognitive responses (i.e., "That's a biased statement") or counterarguments. Stevenson and Greene (1980) have demonstrated this empirically by having respondents indicate on a sheet of text points at which they had stopped mentally to agree or disagree with the content. Readers of biased material were far more likely to make evaluations of content (either to agree or disagree) than readers of unbiased material; readers of biased material were more likely to question or disagree with material than agree with it. While not totally supportive of counterargumentation, this study demonstrated that material that is biased generates more cognitive responses than unbiased material.

In short, both perspectives imply that users tend to overlook the material they agree with and are offended by the material they disagree with, consequently not noticing that on the whole the report is balanced. This was demonstrated empirically when a group of students were presented with dummy newspaper articles that were carefully designed to be balanced on a point-by-point basis. On each of three issues relevant to students (on-campus parking, campus construction, and politics) two points in favor of the students' position and two points opposed, selected from pretests conducted earlier, were presented in the stimulus articles, along with neutral material. When students were asked to circle material in the stimulus article that they regarded as biased, they overwhelmingly circled the material they disagreed with rather than either the material they agreed with or the neutral material (D'Alessio, 2003).

The hostile media effect is important to the discussion here for two reasons. The first is that it explains why it is that so many people possessed of so many different perspectives have all concluded that the media are biased, even when they are unable to agree on the direction or valence of the bias. More simply, it explains why liberals think the media are conservative and conservatives think the media are liberal. While there are news media outlets that can be one or the other, "the media" as an aggregated whole cannot be both liberal and conservative simultaneously across all issues. Instead, liberal users focus on conservative elements of a news media report and conservatives on liberal elements, leading each to claim bias. Since the principle of journalistic fairness requires that both sides be represented, there is always something for people to point at and call "biased."

Secondly, it also has to be noted that among the people susceptible to the hostile media effect can be the people doing the research themselves. The subjective nature of the perception, and consequently the detection, of media bias means that one of the critical questions that surrounds the examination of bias in the media is the question of measurement: how does one "measure" bias? This difficulty is manifest in one of the major attempts to codify bias in the media, Edith Efron's *The News Twisters*. Efron (1971) attempted to measure bias by simply counting statements in the television network newscasts that were pro-liberal or pro-conservative. Unfortunately, instead of proceeding from a neutral standpoint, Efron was attempting to use her data to demonstrate a liberal bias in the news, and unintentionally focused on material she saw as hostile. Her conclusion, that there was a substantial liberal bias, merely reflected her belief that, as a conservative, the media were hostile to her position. When the same study was repeated using formal scientific procedures designed to minimize the role of subjectivity in the results, Efron's conclusions were found to be incorrect (Stevenson et. al, 1973).

CONTENT ANALYSIS

The routine social scientific solution to the subjective nature of media bias is to attempt to move it from the realm of individual opinion to a set of judgments that are, if not objective, then at least intersubjective, which is to say that multiple observers can all agree on the evaluation. Thus the judgment in question is no longer "a cross-section of one man's opinion" (a quip attributed to composer Ken Darby in Kinney, 1988, p. 156).

A common method of creating intersubjectivity is by the use of formal content analysis (Krippendorf, 2003). To do this, a set of content rules is defined, coders are trained in the application of the rules, and then content is not judged in terms of the coders' gestalt opinions but in terms of whether or not they fit the defined content rules. This judging is done by multiple coders so that the extent of agreement in application of the rules can be measured; if there is insufficient agreement, the rules are presumed defective and they are improved.

Empirically speaking, the rule sets for measuring partisan bias in news media reports tend to fall into one of three groups (D'Alessio & Allen, 2006), although it is not uncommon for researchers to consider multiple groups of them in the same study. The first group is what we have come to term "volumetric" biases, because they are concerned primarily with the amount (or volume) of coverage one side or the other gets, with no regard to evaluating the content of the coverage. Thus, researchers have considered, for instance, the number of stories about a campaign, the number of headlines about a campaign, the total running time of TV reports about a campaign, the number and size of photographs of a campaigner, and so on.

The second group of content analytic measurements routinely made about political campaign coverage involve the evaluation of the content in question as to whether it is favorable to one campaign or the other, unfavorable to one or the other, or, in some cases, neutral vis-á-vis both campaigns. Thus, we see researchers examining news reports on a story-by-story or statement-by-statement basis, evaluating whether a story or statement is pro, con, or neutral to one side or another. We term this type of measure to be one of the "valence" of coverage, although it is also frequently called "tone."

A much smaller body of literature attempts to determine the number of newsworthy events opposing campaigns generate, and then looking to see the extent to which the stories of one campaign or the other are broadly reported. Since this is a matter of whether a writer selects to report the story and/or an editor selects to run the story, we call this a "selection" bias if one campaign's stories are disproportionately favored over another's.

To distinguish the three types of bias, let us consider four stories that are available for use in a given news media outlet on one given day during the campaign. The content of the four stories boils down to: "Candidate A is a Bad Person": "Candidate A is a Neutral Person": "Candidate B is a Neutral Person": and "Candidate B is a Good Person." Let us stipulate that content analysis has demonstrated the first story to be negative in valence toward Candidate A while the fourth is positive in valence toward Candidate B. The other two are coded as neutral

If an editor runs all four stories, from the standpoint of volume of coverage he or she has run two stories about each campaign and so coverage is arguably balanced. The same is true if only one story from each side is run, regardless of which of the stories on either side that was selected, or if none of the four stories is run. From the standpoint of volume, any odd number of stories run (one story for one side and two stories for the other, or none for one and one for the other) creates an unbalance that favors the side for which the extra story has been run. (Obviously, two from one side and none from the other would also be considered biased.)

On the other hand, if all four stories are run, from the standpoint of valence an editor who runs all the stories has shown an unbalance favoring Candidate B, since he has run one story that is pro-B, a second that is anti-A (and so presumably also pro-B), and two that are neutral. The means by which the editor's news media outlet would be able to balance the valence of coverage given the body of those four, and only those four, specific stories would be to report only the two neutral stories, or to report none of the four.

An unbalance in selection would be shown by selecting none or one of the stories on one side while taking both on the other, regardless of the valence of the stories in question. Balanced selection would consist of taking the same number of stories from each side, regardless of which of the stories was omitted if only one per side is taken.

As the simplistic example above implies, there is potential for a strain between measures of volumetric and measures of selection bias. In the case where one campaign is genuinely less active than the other, in order to have the same number of articles about each side a news media outlet would have to use proportionately more stories from the less active campaign. This would create a selection bias favoring that campaign. However, we do not consider this problematic in that it points up the advantage of examining as many types of bias as possible in order to have as clear a picture of the actual coverage as possible.

As the example above also suggests, value, volume and selection are taken as separate possible measures of unbalance because of the possibility that they have different messages to convey. Dalton, Beck and Huckfeldt (1998) showed, among a large number of other things, that in 1992 the Bush campaign got a great deal more coverage than the Clinton campaign, that is, the volume of coverage was in favor of the Bush campaign. However, a great deal more of the commentary about the Bush campaign was negative in tone, leading to an unbalance in valence that favored the Clinton campaign. Separating these types of bias will enable us to examine these kinds of statements and allow a greater degree of precision in our conclusions.

ANALYTIC PROCEDURES

I intend to answer the research questions raised at the end of chapter 2 by using the techniques of meta-analysis, which is basically the aggregation of the results of a large number of studies to form a single, overall conclusion that encompasses all of them (Rosenthal, 1991; Hunter & Schmidt, 1990). The analytic procedure itself is fairly straightforward: relevant studies are located, their results converted to a common metric, and the ensuing converted measurements subjected to formal statistical test. As will be seen, the statistical tests themselves are fairly straightforward and easily calculated. The procedural difficulties lie in the locations of relevant studies in a manner that does not influence the ultimate conclusions, and in the conversion of the results of a widely disparate set of studies to a single common metric.

The nature of the search for relevant studies points up immediately two of the advantages of meta-analytic reviews over traditional types of literature review and summation. The first is that traditional, narrative-type reviews rarely consider bodies of literature this exhaustive because they simply cannot; there are simply too many studies here to be reviewed for anyone to make coherent sense of all of them by examining them one study at a time. Some form of aggregation is necessary simply to make sense of that enormous amount of data. Reviewers have attempted to make sense of large numbers of studies by means of the so-called counting review, wherein the number of studies on one side of an issue or the other are simply counted, but this presupposes that all studies are equal and all differences in results are the same (that is, that one study showing a 2:1 advantage is the same as a second study showing a 6:1 advantage). Neither of these presuppositions is necessarily true, as Hunter, Schmidt, and Jackson (1982), have demonstrated.

By aggregating studies, however, we can summarize a large body of data and in turn make use of a second advantage of meta-analysis: the ability to compress the work of what would be several lifetimes worth of work, if it were done by a single researcher, into a single study. Meta-analysis is an example of what is termed "secondary analysis," which means that in most cases it is a re-examination of data previously made public. In the case of the examination of political campaign coverage, the use of content analysis techniques can be slow and time-consuming. It may take a team of researchers months to aggregate and code the content of, for instance, all the nightly network news broadcasts which took place during a given campaign. Once this task has been completed and the results placed on public display, however, the findings of each study of that sort can be placed into the context of the results of numerous other studies performed by other researchers or performed at other times. Further, once the results are placed on public display, for the most part they also become permanently available. The results obtained by researchers who are no longer active can be combined with those generated by scholars fresh out of school because they are all available in libraries, in academic journals, or on the Internet. Indeed, the body of research examined here includes studies made public anywhere from 1949 to 2011.

Because of the exhaustive nature of the literature search and the use of conversion of results to a common metric, meta-analysis is generally considered to be superior to standard methods of literature for three additional, mathematical reasons. First, the use of a common metric for the results allows statistical testing of conclusions. This allows us to distinguish systematic regularities in data from the workings of random chance. Second, the aggregation of large numbers of studies has the statistical consequence of reducing sampling error, which is to say, the potential for error that can arise when samples (or subsets) are drawn from larger populations for study (Hunter & Schmidt, 1990). The possibility of sampling error can be seen, for instance, in the research on coverage conducted on newspapers. In some studies, the content of as few as a single newspaper is used as a surrogate for the actions of all newspapers. Clearly, combining studies of multiple newspapers will lead to superior conclusions. And third, it is possible to test the accumulated studies for homogeneity; that is, to reach or reject the conclusion that external variables break the set of findings into distinct subsets (Hunter, Schmidt & Jackson, 1982). A heterogeneous set of findings is a key sign to the researcher that some external factor is operating on the data. It may not necessarily be found or known, or even of interest, but at least the researcher is aware that it exists.

To accumulate a database of studies that is as comprehensive as possible, a thorough literature search must be conducted. This can include, but is not limited to, searching computerized databases using a number of different search terms; making manual searches of the contents of relevant journals; and examining programs from the professional conferences in the relevant field. In addition, when relevant articles are obtained, their reference sections are in turn searched for leads to more materials. The search is not limited to published journals but can also include theses and unpublished studies if the research is done using an appropriate methodology. Failure to be as comprehensive as possible can systematically bias the results, as Levine and Asada (2007) have demonstrated.

As mentioned earlier, meta-analytic procedures call for the conversion of results to a common metric so that they can be aggregated across studies. There are any number of possible common metrics, but the preferred measures are those that possess a minimum of two characteristics. The first is that the metric in question should not be a function of sample size. Different studies can have different sample sizes, depending on the procedures used by the researchers, making aggregation of these difficult and interpretation problematic if the metric is dependent on sample size. The second is that the chosen metric should be easy to understand and interpret. It is much more useful to have a number that is meaningful on its face than one whose meaning has to be interpreted by the researcher for the audience, or by reference to a table, computer program or other external source.

To this end we have chosen the d' statistic. As defined by Rosenthal (1991), d' is simply the difference between two proportions. In this specific application, if coverage is 60 percent concerned with the Republican candidate and 40 percent with the Democratic, then

$$d' = .40 - .60 = -.20$$

(Note: For the purposes of consistency, unbalances in coverage favoring the Democrats have been arbitrarily coded as positive in sign, except in the cases of certain of the analyses in chapter 5. This is not a requirement of the analytical system, except that one side has to be positive.) d' is not a function of sample size, and in interpretation is readily convertible to percentages (e.g., the $-.20$ calculated above implies a pro-Republican bias of 20 percentage points). Since d' meets our criteria for a common metric, the results of each study will be converted to proportions and the proportions to d'.

Aggregating d' across studies requires that each d' be weighted as a function of the number of the news media outlets it summarizes. As a general rule, statistics calculated from larger numbers of data are more accurate than those calculated from smaller sample sizes, and so those from larger samples are weighted somewhat more heavily than those from smaller samples, as in:

$$\text{Avg } d' = \Sigma\, w_i d'_i / \Sigma\, w_i$$

where $w_i = n_i / (1 - d'^2_i)$, with n_i being the number of news media outlets in the sample. By use of this formula we can calculate an overall, aggregate d' for a number of studies.

The other statistic needed for meta-analysis is some measure of homogeneity, as mentioned previously. This is provided by

$$\chi^2(i\text{-}1) = \Sigma\, w_i\,(d'_i - \text{avg } d')^2$$

or the weighted squared deviations between the average d' and that calculated for each study. As the formula implies, this is distributed as chi-square with degrees of freedom equal to i (the number of studies represented by the calculation) minus one.

THE MEASUREMENT OF MEDIA BIAS

As has been shown, the concept of media bias is both subjective and poorly defined. As a result of these problems, there is no particular agreement as to standard methods of measuring bias, leading to debate in the field as to the meaning or interpretation of the outcome of various studies (not necessarily a bad thing), and to the deployment of a variety of methodologies of potentially greater or lesser utility in answering questions about media bias.

Niven (2002) has conducted several studies using an ingenious methodology wherein media coverage of political figures of systematically differing characteristics is examined when the figures are faced with similar objective circumstances. For instance, he determined that white mayors of major cities received better coverage in their local newspapers than black mayors by comparing press reports on the mayors during periods of similar changes in the local murder rates, that is, when the murder rate had increased 10 percent or more, or declined 5 to 9 percent, and so on, for a total of seven categories of change in murder rate. For six of the seven categories media coverage portrayed white mayors as being more effective than blacks, and the coverage in the seventh category did not differ significantly. Similarly he was able to demonstrate biases against female and black congresspersons by examining press reactions to the involvement of the congressperson in the House banking scandal (in which it was shown that certain congressmen had made a habit of cashing bad checks at the House bank). Blacks and women were more likely to have their involvement in the banking scandal mentioned in stories about them than white and male members of Congress.

Niven examined partisan bias by considering press coverage of the George H. W. Bush and Clinton presidencies under conditions of similar economic news, specifically, matching unemployment rates, and found that there was basically no difference between the coverage that the two received, with the exception that President Clinton was somewhat more likely to be mentioned in stories about the unemployment rate than President Bush. Similar comparisons were constructed for Democratic and Republican governors, mayors and congresspersons, and on the whole there were no more than minimal differences in coverage received by politicians of the opposing parties, leading Niven to the conclusion that "There is simply no evidence for partisan bias" (p. 93).

The problem with this methodology is not demonstrated by its conclusion of partisan bias in this last study. There are legitimate reasons to expect no (or minimal) partisan biases, as has been shown in chapter 2, and consequently the result of no difference in coverage can reasonably be interpreted as evidence of a lack of partisan bias. The problem is clearer in the earlier findings of bias against blacks and women. Each of these two groups received significantly poorer coverage than whites and males, but what is the proper interpretation of that? Is coverage of white males balanced and coverage of blacks and women negative? Is coverage of all candidates positive but just less so in the cases of blacks and women? Is coverage of all candidates negative, with that of blacks and women being the most negative?

As we have seen, a bias is a systematic deflection from some absolute standard. In formal terms, measurements made in the manner Niven deploys are not measured against an absolute standard and so should be described as relative rather than absolute. A systematic difference in press coverage between two groups detected in this manner can be said to be reasonable proof of the existence of a bias somewhere, but makes no statement, and can make no statement, as to whether coverage of the one group or the other, or both, is unbiased. The system detects that there is a bias somewhere, but it is unable to say where.

Another relativistic measurement scheme is proposed by Groseclose and Milyo (2005), who worked inductively from the Americans for Democratic Action (ADA) scores of elected representatives. The ADA score is based on the voting record of the representative in question on specific issues selected by the ADA that are closely tied to the ideological liberal/conservative continuum. Groseclose and Milyo first created a continuum of think tanks (such as the American Enterprise Institute) often used as sources by media outlets, and then, by examining citations to those think tanks in various media outlets, were able to estimate ADA scores for those outlets. This yielded some results that might be described as "expected" given common assumptions regarding the media. For instance, Fox News and the *Washington Times* received conservative scores and *The News York Times*, *Los Angeles Times* and *Washington Post* received liberal scores. On the other hand, the method showed the pro-business *Wall Street Journal* as the most liberal news media outlet examined, by over 10 points on a 100-point scale.

The ADA scoring system possesses face validity, that is, appears to reasonably measure ideological position, in that congresspersons widely regarded as liberal (e.g, Maxine Waters, D-CA; Ted Kennedy, D-MA) typically score higher than congresspersons widely regarded as conservative (Tom Delay, R-TX; Bill Frist, R-TN), and the average Democrat gets a substantially higher score than the average Republican. However, the scoring system is not pegged to any formal, absolute standard. The scale is constructed such that the average voter in a given time epoch would be given a score of 50, but the positions of voters have changed over time, as the ADA's own data indicates (as does Smith, 1990). The ADA's scale also focuses on key issues that distinguish the ends of the spectrum, giving those votes undue weight and exaggerating the distance between points on the scale, particularly toward the center of the scale. Again, in the absence of at least one absolute point against which to measure, while it is possible with this methodology to say one outlet is more or less conservative than another (which, as above, indicates that there is some bias in reporting somewhere), one cannot state for certain that one news media outlet is biased and another is not.

Yet another approach to measuring media bias follows from the examination of media bias in several European nations. In particular, since broadcast media in, for instance, the Scandinavian nations are more closely associated with the government than they are in United States, the political nature of broadcast news outlets as channels for information from candidates to the voters is more carefully monitored than it is in the United States.

In the United Kingdom the media are charged with reporting the news "objectively." To some of the researchers, such as Gunter (1997) and Westerhahl (1983), who have been charged with evaluating media performance, the notion of "objectivity" encompasses four factors grouped into two major areas. First, there is the question of factuality, which implies that the "facts" related in a story must be both correct and accurate; and second, there is the question of impartiality, which subsumes the dual notions of neutrality and balance.

This type of approach has two advantages from our point of view. First, it is a better and more complete definition of what constitutes media performance in the coverage of an issue such as a political campaign. Second, it implies a measurement scheme that includes the type of absolute point against which an amount of bias can be measured.

If we examine the components of the approach, for our purposes the notion of factuality is presupposed. A news media outlet that cannot keep its facts straight on a routine basis is subject to civil action if the information is perceived as defamatory, and runs the risk of loss of credibility, arguably followed by loss of users and loss of advertising revenue. Certainly, credibility is considered vital to the news media (ASNE, 2001) and so it is in a news media outlet's best interests to keep its facts straight.

When discussing the nature of impartiality as being a function of balance and neutrality, it seems reasonable to argue that in some ways these two concepts are closely related. Balance, for instance, implies that the various sides associated with an issue receive equal coverage in terms of volume, while neutrality implies that, to the extent news media outlets inject evaluation and opinion into news content, that they do so without favoring either side. In other words, so far as discussions of bias are concerned, the goal of a news media outlet is to have equal coverage for both sides and to be as critical of one side as the other. Mathematically, this implies that the measurement of bias, d', should be 0 for both volumetric measures and measures of valence. Since fairness and balance are also explicitly regarded as ethical responsibilities of news media outlets (as discussed in chapter 2), for the purposes of the research performed herein, we will assume that the extent of a news media outlet's degree of bias is measured by the amount of deviation of d' from 0.

This assumption has been criticized historically by scholars (e.g., Kobre, 1953; Niven, 2002) who have pointed out that it is distinctly possible that, in a given campaign for office, one campaigner may simply generate more news than the other. This would imply in turn that so-called balanced coverage is actually an unfair and inappropriate goal. If one campaign generates 60 percent of the news in a campaign, then accurate reporting should reflect this fact, as discussed earlier. There is some merit to this reasoning. For instance, during the 1980 presidential campaign, beset by a bad economy and the plight of U.S. citizens being held captive by Iranian radicals, President Carter undertook what came to be called a "Rose Garden" campaign strategy. He attempted to present himself to the public as preoccupied by his duties and therefore less available to campaign than his opponent, Ronald Reagan (c.f. Hauser, 1999). It is not unreasonable to expect that the Carter campaign generated a lesser volume of news than the Reagan campaign (once Carter's activities as president were eliminated from the analysis), leading to negative (or pro-Republican) d's simply because Carter did less campaigning.

As appealing as this reasoning is on the face of it, we have to reject it for several reasons. First, the activity or inactivity of a given campaign is not necessarily tied to a specific party or ideology. Instead, campaign activity should be distributed more or less randomly across parties, and so the net effect in the aggregate should be zero. In other words, should there be a Democratic campaign in one election that generates less news, it is just as likely that in another election a Republican campaign might be the one that does less. Activity is unrelated to party, so while this idea could be valuable in considering a single campaign, it is less valuable for examining multiple campaigns as we do here.

Second, it is worth noting that we are not inventing the notion of balance as a goal in the news coverage of an election herein; rather, it is a goal that has been created by the industry itself. It can be seen explicitly, for instance, in the decisions of the *Los Angeles Times* in covering the 1962 gubernatorial race, as discussed in chapter 1, and in the codes of conduct promulgated by organizations such as the Associated Press, Scripps-Howard newspapers and the Society for Professional Journalists. Fairness and balance are not only goals set by regulatory agencies in Europe; they are outcomes that the industry expects of itself.

Finally, to argue that coverage need not be balanced because one campaign may generate more news than another begs the related and interrelated questions of "What is news?" and "Who decides what news is?" It should be evident that it is a simple matter for a news reporter to counter charges of biased reporting by simply responding, "I am not biased. What that campaign is doing is not news." The phrase missing from that statement, of course, would be "in my subjective opinion," and since it is our purpose here to try and measure things objectively (or at least intersubjectively), we are therefore more or less required to reject this argument. In logical terms, to argue, "I covered one campaign less because it was my opinion that it was less newsworthy" is to engage in tautology: it is the logical equivalent of saying "I am right because I am right."

Stempel (2011) suggests a possible solution to correcting for the amount of news generated by campaigns that relies on looking at independent news media outlets and those whose editorial positions are at odds with their news reporting. A paper aligned with the Democratic party whose coverage is pro-Democratic is clearly an instance of bias (and the same for Republican papers favoring Republicans). But if independent papers are showing consistent volumetric biases that also match up with those of papers whose coverage doesn't match their editorial preferences, this can be said to be clear evidence that one campaign was simply more active. Certainly it is as good an explanation of these observations as imputing ideological biases would be.

For example, if we have a Democratic paper, a Republican paper and an independent paper, if their measures of volumetric bias all agree, then it seems likely that this result is a consequence of campaign activity rather than ideological bias in operation. Were the coverages a consequence of ideological bias, then we would expect to see the Democratic paper favoring the Democrat, the Republican paper the Republican and the independent paper roughly balanced. The value of this methodology would be that it would provide an ad hoc means of correcting volumetric bias for the impact of campaign activity.

While valuable, use of a technique of this sort is dependent on the reliable identification of a news media outlet as Republican, Democratic or independent. In some cases, such as that of the *Chicago Tribune*, this is a straightforward determination. The *Tribune* has supported Republican presidential candidates exclusively for at least the last sixty years. In other cases, however, this assignment is less obvious. For instance, the *Boston Globe* is generally regarded as a Democratic paper, but until 1984 the *Globe* did not endorse presidential candidates, giving the outward appearance of independence. Similarly, the *Wall Street Journal* still does not endorse candidates, despite a general preference for pro-business, Republican, policies. Until a reliable method of determining the political identity of a news media outlet apart from their preferences in coverage and editorial endorsement is found, this will be unworkable for us to use herein, since in most cases the only information available are the measurements of coverage (d') and the outlet's endorsement for president.

Thus, we are left with the standard of balanced reporting across all the possible types of bias—volumetric, valence, and selection—as measured using the d' statistic, expecting that balanced reporting would be represented as $d' = 0$. We recognize that this is a goal state to be striven for but which, given the precision of measurement possible, might never be achieved by the coverage of any one news media outlet. We further recognize that consistent and persistent deviations from $d' = 0$ indicate partisan media bias as we have defined it, favorable to the party indicated by the sign of d', with d' greater than zero indicating a pro-Democratic (and presumably liberal) bias and d' less than zero indicating a pro-Republican (and presumably conservative) bias. In chapter 4 we will look at the question of bias in the aggregate, across media and across time.

4

Are "The Media" "Biased"?

The large question is, "Are the media biased?" It should be evident from chapter 2 in particular that the answer to a question that broad has to be "Yes." The complex set of socioeconomic roles media outlets must fill necessitates that any given outlet, not to mention the entire industry as a whole, shows consistent regularities in content. For example, as mentioned previously, Page and Shapiro (1992) assert that there is a pro-democracy bias in the U.S. news media industries, and it is self-evident that this be true.Non-democratic political systems impose restrictions on the media industries that are contradictory to their needs, and thus as a matter of self-interest American media industries demonstrate a preference for democratic systems, that is, a bias.

It should also be clear from the multiple natures of news media industries that there is a large number of such biases, most of them for the most part transparent to the industries, users and critics alike. For instance, few Americans would seriously advocate that the news be presented by a single government agency. It is preferable to the vast majority of interested parties that news reporting come from outlets that are both pluralistic and competitive in nature. A point source for news would also constitute a point source for censorship and disinformation while a pluralistic, competitive system works to prevent restrictions in the flows of critical information to the public. As a consequence of that, not to mention the financial interests of the owners of news media outlets, mediated opinion on the topic would oppose the presentation of news by a single government agency, and would do so with almost perfect unanimity. This would also constitute a bias as we have defined it.

It should also be evident that to attempt to answer the broad question "Are the media biased?" empirically would be a task beyond what can be accomplished in a single research study and within the confines of a single book. People have attempted to approach the question from the standpoint of logical analysis supported by specific examples before, but as we have seen, reasoning in this way is subject to the difficulties raised by the concepts of confirmation bias and the hostile media effect. To avoid these problems in this volume necessitates narrowing the broad question as to whether the media are biased to something more manageable.

More specific (and incidentally more interesting) questions are "Do the media have a liberal bias?" and "Do the media have a conservative bias?" As we have also seen, there are legitimate reasons inherent in the nature of news media industry structures sufficient to allow us to support an answer of "Yes" to either in the absence of empirical evidence. "Yes," there are reasons, based particularly on the journalistic nature of the news media, to expect a liberal bias in the news; "Yes," there are reasons, based on the business and property natures of the news media, to expect a conservative bias in the news.

In either case we are examining the possibility of an ideological bias along the "left/liberal" and "right/conservative" axis of political thought. Unfortunately, there are innumerable issues—civil rights, foreign affairs, religious and moral questions, business practices, taxation and many more—that can be analyzed along that axis, and so to simply consider the broad question of ideological bias generally again leaves us with an unmanageably large task to be undertaken in one volume by empirical analysis.

On the other hand, considering the question of ideological bias in news media outlets during political campaigns, particularly campaigns for president of the United States, is a manageable task. First, there have been only a limited number of presidential elections and thus presidential election campaigns—fifty-six since the founding of the republic—and a number of these campaigns can be eliminated from analysis simply because the nature of the news media and their role in the campaign process has irrevocably changed in the decades since they were conducted (Stebenne, 1993). Second, ideological bias can be simply estimated with a certain degree of accuracy by examining the much-more-easily measured partisan bias because of the general association of the Republican Party with the ideological right and the Democrats with the left. This is not a one-to-one association, as party platforms and positions have shifted across time due to changes in philosophy and/or the exigencies of need, but the association between party and ideology is sufficiently large to allow us to use party as a surrogate for ideology.

From a mechanical standpoint, choosing the performance of media news outlets in the coverage of presidential campaigns has several other advantages. First, each party nominates a candidate who is at least minimally qualified for the highest nation in the land. Of the major party presidential candidates nominated since Franklin Roosevelt's terms in office, only one had previously not served in one or more of the positions of vice president, U.S. Senator or state governor, and that one was Dwight Eisenhower, a retired five-star general who had been Supreme Commander of the European Theater of Operations during World War II and the first commander of NATO. Further, every presidential candidate has passed through a nominating process meant not simply to produce a qualified candidate, but more importantly a candidate who is capable of winning the general election. This is not to argue that all candidates are created equal, but simply to make the point that no unqualified candidates have been nominated, and media coverage of their campaigns should reflect this relative balance.

And second, the value of considering the possibility of media bias in presidential elections is magnified by the importance of the outcome of the process. The election as currently constructed is a "winner-take-all" event: the winner becomes the leader of the free world and the loser gets nothing. While there have been lopsided, landslide elections in the post–World War II era, there have also been several, including the elections of 1960 and 2000, decided by the electoral votes of a single state and thus by a relatively small handful of voters. If the outcomes of these elections are traceable to biases in reporting in the media, then the effect of biased media reporting on a relatively small number of voters has a potentially large consequence for both the nation and the world.

From the standpoint of meta-analysis, which is the analytic method chosen for this report, the importance of presidential campaigns implies that they are frequently the focus of scientific study. As pointed out, meta-analysis is conducted on a body of literature that has already accumulated; it follows reasonably that important and consequential issues are studied more frequently than trivial or obscure ones. The larger the body of literature available for analysis, the greater the number of hypotheses that can be explored, and the greater our confidence in the conclusions that can be drawn from testing those hypotheses. Media coverage of presidential election campaigns has been studied repeatedly, using a variety of methodologies, in the 1948 to 2008 period, and so the question of coverage of presidential election campaigns is one that might be approached in the hope of gaining intellectual profit.

EXAMINING CAMPAIGN COVERAGE

As just stated, there have been a number of studies of the media coverage of U.S. presidential campaigns. As a rule, they fall into several primary categories. First, there are studies of voting and the individual decisions regarding selecting a candidate (e.g., Berelson, Lazarsfeld & McPhee, 1954). As media inputs are considered to be one of the factors influencing the votes of individuals, the examination of media content is necessary to estimating the magnitude of that influence. These studies can include the examination of the content of a number of news media outlets in a number of different media, as part of a general measurement of the news and opinion content milieu surrounding the decisions being made.

A second group of studies is interested in the structural characteristics of reporting of campaigns by news media outlets (c.f. Benoit et al., 2005; CMPA, 2009). This can include elements such as the proportion of coverage devoted to issues as opposed to poll results or the "horse race" of the campaign, or the "play" that each campaign receives in terms of the number of photographs, the size of headlines, the location of stories early or late in a newscast and so on. These are of value to our study in that among these structural elements of news coverage of a campaign can be the amount (volume) or tone (valence) of coverage accorded to the campaigns of the different parties. This group can also include cross-media comparisons, in order to examine the differences in structure and coverage between media.

Finally, there are studies explicitly intended to examine partisan bias in media coverage, or related phenomena such as fairness and balance (e.g., Blumberg, 1954; Fico & Cote, 1999). These studies generally consider only one medium at a time, but the content of newspapers (Stempel, 1961), newsmagazines (Moriarty & Garramone, 1987), televised news from both networks (Frank, 1973) and local television stations (Pritchard, 2002), radio (Terry, 2005), and even such ephemeral media as editorial cartoons (Thalheimer, 1993) and late night talk TV (Niven, Lichter & Amundson, 2003) have been examined at one time or another.

The results of these studies can be highly variable depending on the electoral campaign(s) being examined, the exact news media outlets being studied, the type of bias or media content of interest, and the exact methodology being deployed. Conclusions can range from the belief that the media are highly favorable to the Republicans (e.g., Graber, 1976), highly favorable to the Democrats (e.g., Clancey & Robinson, 1985) or reasonably well balanced within the limits of the methodology being used (e.g., Doll & Bradley, 1974). Sometimes studies of the same media coverage of the same campaign can lead to contradictory conclusions, which probably says more about the influence of the individual researcher's techniques than about the body of content itself.

For the most part, these studies consider a single election campaign or, at most, two consecutively. This is not unexpected given the nature of academic life and the period of years between each campaign. The exceptions are retrospective studies meant to examine changes in coverage over some given period of time. These include Batlin's (1954) comparison of the San Francisco papers' coverage of the 1896 and 1952 campaigns, and Benoit et al.'s (2005) structural analysis of *The New York Times* coverage of campaigns from the 1950s to 2004.

Similarly, there are studies that attempt to consider a cross-section of media outlets. Dalton and his colleagues (Dalton, Beck & Huckfeldt, 1998), for instance, selected a number of counties from around the country in order to create a representation of the nation, and within those counties examined the content of each available newspaper, a total of 46 in all. Blumberg (1954) and Graber (1976) also attempted to take representative sets of newspapers from around the nation, selecting thirty-five and twenty respectively.

Other studies consider as few as one or two newspapers, considering them to be representative of the whole due to the prestige accorded to them in the industry, such as *The New York Times* or the *Washington Post* (Hofstetter, 1978), or as being the dominant paper in a particular region under examination (Fisher, 2001).

A particular subset of studies subsumes the work Stempel and his colleagues (Stempel, 1961; Evarts & Stempel, 1974; Stempel & Windhauser, 1989, among others) have done working with the (originally) fifteen papers making up the so-called Prestige Press numerous times since Guido Stempel started the research in 1960. The term "Prestige Press" was coined by Stempel (1961) to refer to the results of a study conducted by *Practical English* magazine that polled newspaper editors as to the identity of newspapers that were "most superior for news coverage, integrity and public service." (*Editor & Publisher*, 1958, p.12) Following multiple rounds of polling, the papers nominated were, in order, *The New York Times, Christian Science Monitor, Milwaukee Journal, St. Louis Post Dispatch, Washington Post, Louisville Courier-Journal, Wall Street Journal, Atlanta Constitution, Chicago Tribune, Des Moines Register, Kansas City Star, Baltimore Sun, Miami Herald, Chicago Daily News* and *Los Angeles Times*. As a result of the interest of this group of researchers, coverage of each of these papers has been examined numerous times ranging from the election of 1960 (Stempel, 1961) to that of 1992 (King, 1995) specifically because of an interest in the performance of the Prestige Press. It must be added that several of these papers, particularly *The New York Times, Washington Post* and *Los Angeles Times*, have been examined in other contexts as well, but in most of the subanalyses presented in chapter 5 the preponderance of studies of the Prestige Press requires that they be examined separately from other papers.

Examinations of television content tend to be more comprehensive in that they tend to consider the offerings of the network newscasts of all three networks. The networked structure of the television industry creates the potential for a much more centralized news hole, and once one has started to examine television news content, it is only somewhat more difficult to examine all three networks than to just select one, although on occasion CBS is chosen as the surrogate for all three networks (e.g., Malaney & Buss, 1979). More recent studies of television coverage of presidential election campaigns have also started to consider national news outlets in competition with the networks, including at various times PBS, CNN, Fox News and MSNBC. Similarly, studies of newsmagazine content generally consider all of the "big three;" that is to say, *Time, Newsweek,* and the *US News and World Report,* and no other magazines.

Historically, as can be seen from figure 4.1, which plots the number of studies of a given election across time, at least in the early days, the examination of media content is arguably driven to a large degree by public accusations of media bias. It was during the 1948 campaign that President Truman made public charges decrying what was called a "one-party press," and when the charges were repeated in 1952 the number of studies of that campaign spiked to eight. (Blumberg's 1954 book was titled *One Party Press?,* for instance.)

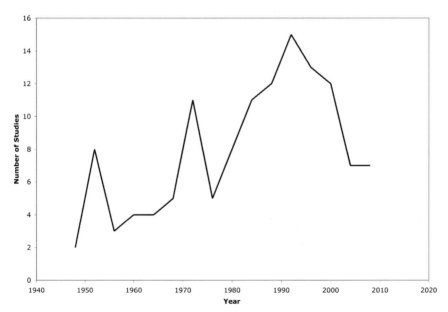

Figure 4.1.   Number of Studies by Year.

Following the 1952 election, the number of studies of press performance declines to a relative handful until the 1972 campaign, which was the first to follow a series of complaints against the media launched by then–vice president Spiro Agnew (1969a, 1969b). Once again the number of studies spiked, this time to eleven, and again the quantity returned to a smaller number until the period of the 1980s, by which time more social scientists were doing more research than ever before. The final peak lies at the 1992 election, noted for the catchphrase "Annoy the media: Re-elect Bush," clearly implying that media coverage again was a bone of contention. The tally falls off at the end, of course, because studies of the last few elections are still in the process of being written, and the studies that will consider these campaigns retrospectively have yet to be conceived.

One particular study that must be considered is our own previous work on this topic (D'Alessio & Allen, 2000). Using the same techniques there that are being used here, we examined the content of 59 studies covering newspaper, network TV and newsmagazine coverage of campaigns from 1948 to 1996, concluding ultimately that "the results indicate an aggregate, across all media and all elections, of zero overall bias (p. 148)."

The present study is an improvement on the earlier one in the following ways:

1. The number of studies has been increased from fifty-nine to ninety-nine by
2. including the 2000, 2004 and 2008 elections,
3. including studies we had not located previously and
4. including studies containing data we had previously been unable to analyze.

Method

We compiled a database of studies, starting with the studies we already had on hand from our 2000 research. We then searched the Internet, particularly Google Scholar, using search terms including "media coverage presidential election," "newspaper coverage presidential election," "media bias presidential election" and the like. As each study was located, its reference section was examined for citations to other studies that might be of interest. Also searched were programs to International Communication Association and National Communication Association conventions and appropriate papers obtained when possible. In this way a database of several hundred studies was recovered.

From that we selected all the studies that met the following criteria:

1. They had to possess formal measurements of media content. Thus, pieces based on narrative reasoning supported by illustrative examples (e.g. Goldberg, 2003) were eliminated due to the possibility of contamination by the process of confirmation bias;
2. Studies had to cover the entire presidential campaign (defined as the period from Labor Day to Election Day of the campaign year) or a substantive part thereof. This eliminated studies that solely examined coverage of the debates, conventions or nominating campaigns (e.g., Hayes & Murray, 1998; Westley et al., 1963), or campaigns at levels below the presidency (Barrett & Barrington, 2005);
3. Measured data had to be separated by party. This eliminated many studies of structural changes in coverage over time and the like (e.g., Hallin, 1992), or studies of how one candidate was covered in isolation from the other (e.g., Fitzgerald, 1995);
4. Measured data had to be meaningfully quantifiable. This excluded studies that focused solely on issues of "play," for instance, or of the structural elements of visual images or the nonverbal behaviors of news anchors (e.g., Babad, 2005; Wortham & Locher, 1996). It may be valuable to know that one candidate is, for instance, more often pictured in close-up than another, but the interpretation of this as being "pro" or "con" is problematic; and
5. Data had to be derived from newspapers, radio, newsmagazines or TV network or cable newscasts. This is a strictly mechanical requirement in that while media such as local television news (e.g., Ostroff & Sandell, 1989) and the Internet (e.g., Kern, 2001) have been studied at times, there is not sufficient information available on those media to draw meaningful conclusions. Similarly, examinations of the Associate Press (e.g., Rucker, 1960) feed were excluded, as individual news media outlets are free to use all, any or none of it as they see fit, or to rewrite copy to meet their needs, and so AP content is of necessity a poor predictor of the content that was actually printed or aired.

One more study was excluded as it failed of replication. When Stevenson et al. (1973) went back over the same data examined by Efron (1971) using the techniques of content analysis described in chapter 3, they arrived at very different conclusions, suggesting that the Efron study was methodologically inadequate.

Once this process was complete, we had located ninety-nine studies that met all the criteria. Each of them was then examined for measurements of the three types of bias discussed in chapter 3: volumetric biases, which relate to the amount of coverage; valence biases, which refer to whether coverage is positive or negative in tone; and selection biases, which is a measurement of the proportion of campaign stories picked up by news media outlets on a per party basis. In print outlets volumetric measurements can be based on either the number of items or the aggregate size (or amount) of items. It is not impossible for one campaign to engender fewer but longer stories than another, or fewer but larger photographs. Measurements of number could include such things as the number of stories about a campaign, the number of photographs published, the number of headlines referring to the campaign or the number of statements made about the campaign. Measurements of amount include such things as the size of photographs or print stories measured in column inches or televised stories measured in terms of seconds, minutes or hours, or lines of copy.

Measures of valenced coverage require an evaluation of whether the content is positive or negative toward a given campaign. Many researchers also include a category for items that are evaluated to be neutral in valence. Studies of valence of content, too, can be further be broken down by the same number/amount distinction made for measurements of volumetric bias. For instance, the number of positive, negative or neutral statements printed (or spoken on TV) about a campaign, as opposed to the composite length of stories adjudged to be for or against a given campaign.

The measurement of selection bias requires the establishment of a baseline number of events generated by each campaign, and then a measurement of the percentage of those stories picked up by news media outlets per party.

The results of each study were converted to the d' statistic described in chapter 3. For studies measuring volume this was straightforward enough: d' would simply be the proportion of coverage of the Democratic campaign minus the proportion of Republican coverage. Coverage of third party candidates, which was fairly substantial in the 1948 (Henry Wallace and J. Strom Thurmond), 1968 (George Wallace), 1980 (John Anderson), and the 1992 and 1996 (Ross Perot) campaigns, was simply omitted from the calculation. In formal mathematical terms, we were looking at the proportion of coverage divided between the major parties alone.

For the studies of valence, d' was calculated by taking the number of positive content elements about one party and adding those that were judged to be negative toward the other party plus one-half the neutral statements and dividing by the grand total. Following the arbitrary decision to make pro-Democratic coverage positive in sign, we therefore used pro-Democratic plus anti-Republican plus one-half the neutral content elements, be they numbers of stories or minutes of coverage or whatever, minus the anti-Democratic plus pro-Republican plus one-half the neutral content for the calculation of d'.

Selection bias was calculated based on comparing the proportion of Democratic stories used to the proportion of Republican stories used. For studies that used some form of scaled measurement, d' was calculated by adding the scores together to create a total and then dividing that into the Democrat's score, then converting the resulting proportion to d'.

This produced an analysis where the 99 studies that composed the database yielded 210 measures of one or more types of potential media bias. These were compiled into a master analysis table that is too large to be reproduced here, so I have included it as Appendix A, along with full citations to each of the studies referenced by it. Appendix A includes reference to each study included, the news medium results are presented for in the study, the type of bias reported in terms of both type of bias (volume, valence, or selection) and also whether the content was measured in terms of a number of content elements (such as number of stories) or amount of coverage (such as minutes of air time). Also reported for each study is the number of news media outlets examined, the campaign year under examination and the d' calculated for each test. From d' and the number of outlets, w_i can be calculated for each study, and from the results of the individual studies the average d', and the χ^2 measure of homogeneity were calculated as described in chapter 3.

For analytical purposes, an overall d' for all studies across all media and all types of bias was constructed. The purpose of this was to answer the broad question of whether media coverage of presidential election campaigns was biased, presupposing that "media" in this case means "all media." A d' significantly different from zero would indicate an overall bias of some kind, the direction (pro-Democrat and thus presumably liberal or pro-Republican and therefore conservative) determined by the sign of d'.

Of necessity, however, an overall measure subsuming "all media" involves combining measurements of very different things. For instance, newsmagazines and TV network news are essentially national media, while newspapers, with the exceptions of *USA Today* and arguably *The New York Times*, are local media serving their local markets. Similarly, as pointed out in chapter 3, measures of volume and valence are examining characteristics of coverage that are potentially very different. It is not uncommon for one campaign or another to attract a great deal of coverage, more than their opponent, because the media are highly critical of the campaign or the candidate. In such a case, measurements of volume would show a bias toward that campaign while measures of valence would show bias against it (assuming that there was bias shown at all).

To gain a greater understanding of the processes in question, and also to avoid the problem of mixing different media and different types of measurement, we supplemented the overall analysis with separate analyses for newspapers, TV network news and newsmagazines. Within each medium we further broke down the results by whether they were derived from examinations of volume and valence. We also examined selection bias in the newspaper industry (there have been no studies of selection bias in other media).

Results of the Overall Analysis

As shown in table 4.1, the overall (apples and oranges) analysis yielded a d' of $-.017$. In formal scientific terms, this result is not statistically significant, meaning that this result is no larger than could be expected based on the workings of random chance alone. The results are also homogeneous ($\chi^2(209) = 24.6$, n.s.), as per chapter 3, suggesting that the result transcends specific campaigns or media.

In making sense of this finding, and all the subsequent findings, it is first necessary to distinguish between statistical significance and substantive significance. Statistical significance is the statement that it is unlikely (odds of no greater than one in twenty) that simple chance occurrences could have created the results observed. Whenever one is dealing with a subset of data derived from a larger mass, it is possible that, despite following all the proper procedures and doing everything "right," the selected subset might not be representative of the whole, and could themselves yield misleading results. The likelihood of random factors alone causing a given result are expressed as a proportion, p, and in general p's greater than .05 (or one chance in 20) are considered to be nonsignificant, that is, most likely caused by random factors to be considered definitive.

Table 4.1. Overall analysis of bias by medium

			d'	sd	n	t	p
Overall			-017	.141	210	1.92	n.s.
	Newspapers						
		Volume	$-.047$	.133	78	3.12	<.001
		Valence	.048	.126	30	2.09	<.05
		Selection	$-.037$	.088	7	1.11	n.s.
	Television						
		Volume	.006	.123	38	0.30	n.s
		Valence	.067	.174	37	2.34	<.05
	Newsmagazines						
		Volume	$-.036$	.123	9	0.88	n.s.
		Valence	$-.090$	.154	8	1.66	n.s.

Substantive significance refers to the size or the relationship or measurement observed. The question of substantive significance is "Is this measurement large enough to matter?" and the answer to it a matter of opinion and interpretation rather than mathematically measured.

When we consider our overall result, $d' = -.017$, three things stand out immediately:

1. It is statistically nonsignificant, that is, it cannot be distinguished from zero statistically;
2. A d' of $-.017$ means that the breakdown of coverage is roughly 50.9 percent Republican to 49.1 percent Democratic, a differential that is both insubstantial and almost certainly indistinguishable from "perfectly balanced"; and consequently we conclude that
3. There is no evidence of a large, universal liberal media bias. None. Just as we reported in 2000, to the extent of our ability to measure bias, the media as a whole are unbiased in their coverage of presidential election campaigns. Furthermore, it should also be noted that there is no evidence of a large, universal conservative bias, either. On the whole, across all media and all elections, coverage can reasonably be said to have been balanced, and thus presumably fair.

As we discussed above, this overall analysis subsumes different media and different possible sources of bias. It was constructed to respond to the broad claim that "The media are biased." In order to avoid comparing apples to oranges, we can break the results down by medium (newspapers, TV and newsmagazines) and type of bias (volume, valence and selection), and these breakdowns are also presented in table 4.1, thereby constructing measures of bias within studies considering similar media and content.

Across the period of time we have been examining, Republicans have received slightly more coverage than Democrats in newspapers, $d' = -.047$, or a hair less than five percentage points more, which is to say the volume of coverage in newspapers has been about 52.4 percent Republican to 47.6 percent Democratic. This result is statistically significant, ($p < .001$) although again I would have to question the substantive differences. When known processes such as selective exposure (the tendency to choose mediated content that agrees with your preexisting opinions) are taken into account, it is unlikely that people are actually exposed to more content on any side of any issue that they disagree with than they are exposed to content on the side that agrees with them. A d' of .047, regardless of sign, is a difference probably too small to be detected by the average newspaper reader, particularly when one recalls that this difference subsumes coverage in numerous newspapers from all across the nation as opposed to the few available in any given locale.

Only two of the other subgroups have yielded d's statistically significantly different from zero, and those are the tone, or valence, of newspaper coverage ($d' = .048$) and television network news coverage ($d' = .067$). The tone of coverage tended to favor the Democratic candidate in the proportion of roughly 53 percent to 47 percent, somewhat less in newspapers, somewhat more in television. This again begs the question of substance: is this a difference large enough to be either detectable to the average viewer or influential on that viewer? It is clear that the tone of a newscaster's voice/presentation can influence viewers (see Babad, 2005), although no one seems to have examined the impact of the tone of a newspaper article. However, a difference of 53 to 47 is also not a completely one-sided presentation by any stretch of the imagination.

None of the other measurements—those of selection biases in newspapers, of volume of television coverage, and of the volume and valence on newsmagazine coverage—differs statistically from zero. Effectively, these measurements all indicate balanced coverage for each of these combinations of medium and bias type. Most noteworthy of these is the $d' = -.090$ for the valence of newsmagazine coverage, which was the largest of the d's calculated for table 4.1. Although larger in magnitude than the two statistically significant results, this one is nonsignificant (because it is based on a much smaller number of studies), and therefore must be treated as a difference of zero, indicating balanced coverage.

However, it should also be noted that the question of statistical significance is somewhat more problematic when talking about TV network news and newsmagazine content because in some cases the researchers whose studies are contributing to this analysis are not dealing with samples (as is presupposed by the process of statistical testing). Some researchers have chosen to, for instance, examine the news content of only one of the networks to represent the content of all three, or created "composite weeks" of coverage by choosing to examine the content of one network on one day, a second on the next day, and so on, or examining a subset by choosing only coverage from Monday, Wednesdays and Fridays. In each of these cases we are looking at sampling a subset of all the coverage, and the question of statistical significance must be raised.

On the other hand, the amount of TV network news coverage of a given election season is a manageable amount of content, on the average a relatively small number of hours (less than ten) per network per campaign, and a number of researchers have worked with the entire body of content, rather than a subset or sample of it. In these instances the question of statistical sampling or statistical significance is irrelevant. The proportion of coverage measured for one candidate is the proportion they actually got, with no statistical inferences involved.

If we assume that significance testing is irrelevant in cases where researchers have accessed the population of content, then it is possible to argue that TV network news, studies of which at times can also include Fox News, CNN, PBS and MSNBC in their measurements, show a very slight favoritism to the Democrats. It should again be noted that the d' for valence of TV network news, +.067, represents coverage that is 53.4 percent favorable to Democrats and 46.6 percent to Republicans. This again presumes that you watch all the network news on all the networks, which is theoretically possible in the age of TiVo, but unlikely. The volume of coverage also favors the Democrats, by an even smaller amount, $d' = .006$, or a difference of less than 51 percent Democratic to 49 percent Republican. It makes sense that the volume of coverage should be very close to balanced given that for many years TV networks labored under the mandatory Equal Time Provision, which required that candidates get equal volumes of coverage.

Similarly, if we treat newsmagazines as being measurements of populations rather than of samples (again, because researchers can deal with the entire body of content rather than a sample of it), we see a slight favoritism to the Republicans in both volume and tone. Again, this difference is minute, although the valence of newsmagazine coverage is $d' = -.090$, or 54.5 percent favorable to Republicans and 45.5 percent favorable to Democrats. Once again, this is underlain by the assumption that the reader reads *Time*, *Newsweek* and *US News and World Report* weekly, which is less unlikely than the notion of watching all three TV network newscasts daily. Conclusions regarding the coverage newsmagazines give to campaigns must also be regarded as being tentative due to the small number of studies of them conducted, and also because of the relatively large proportion of studies that focus solely on photographic elements of coverage.

If one assumes that the statistical tests are the equivalent of flipping a coin, the signs of the d's are as even as an odd number of signs can be: four negative and three positive. This, too, is inconsistent with the idea of a monolithic bias in favor of either party.

In short, to the extent of our ability to measure media content, media coverage of presidential election campaigns appears to be fairly well balanced. Republicans have a small edge in the volume of coverage in newspapers and, arguably, in the newsmagazines; Democrats in the tone of coverage. None of the differences is large, and the homogeneity of the data—all of the subsets are shown to be homogeneous by the χ^2 test described in chapter 3—suggests that this balance is generally true from election to election and candidate to candidate.

This conclusion does *not* mean that every news media outlet is fair and unbiased in its campaign coverage and in fact we know that there are outlets who clearly fall on either end of the ideological spectrum, with obvious implications concerning partisan biases. As we have seen in chapter 2, people buy or start news media outlets for any number of reasons, some of them ideological. Under those conditions it is reasonable to assume that the outlet in question serves the ideological needs of the founder/owner. One presumes that if it did not, he or she would arrange for it to be so!

Therefore, based on the results of this analysis I am not claiming that all news media outlets are unbiased, even in partisan terms. We have yet to look at news media outlets individually. But the data clearly indicate that *on the whole*, for the most part the media are neither pro-Republican, nor pro-Democrat; nether conservative, nor liberal. There is certainly no evidence of a monolithic bias in the favor of either end of the political spectrum engendered by the political beliefs of either journalists or owners.

There is no evidence that news media outlets act in unison as a monopoly or a monolith, but at the same time we know that individual news media outlets can be biased, and, in fact, suspect that some of them are. That said, we are again led to the question: What factors influence the partisan (and by implication, ideological) biases of a specific news media outlet? This is the question to be pursued in chapter 5.

5

Myths and Realities of Coverage

It is one thing to say that there is no evidence of an aggregate partisan bias in the media. As we pointed out at the end of the last chapter, however, it is another thing entirely to say that there is no bias in the media. As we have seen, I could, for instance, point to examples of specific news media outlets that I believe to be biased based on my personal observations of them. Unfortunately for me, at the same time my personal observations are as susceptible to instance confirmation and the hostile media effect as anyone else's.

Still, at the same time, if one looks at the general tendencies of individual outlets, oftentimes outlets serving the same media market who are each supposedly serving an audience of a given ideology, it is clear that the coverage of one is more politically conservative or liberal than the other. Washington has her *Post*, reputedly one of the most liberal newspapers in the nation, and the *Times*, specifically founded to speak with a conservative voice (United Press International, 1982). Boston has the *Globe* and the *Herald*; New York the *Times* and the *Post*; Chicago the *Tribune* and (basically) everyone else. For many years, until they were combined in a Joint Operating Agreement, there were the *Detroit News* and the *Detroit Free Press*. And there are numerous other examples. In short, while "the media" may not be biased, there are clearly biased media outlets.

In fact, the result of no *aggregate* partisan bias can easily be achieved even in the presence of substantial amounts of partisan bias in the media. Put simply, you can reach the conclusion that the media are balanced on the whole under conditions where either a) there is no partisan bias or b) news media outlets favoring Republicans are offset by outlets preferring Democrats. While is it presumed that the economics of mass media systems will favor a centrist orientation, it is unlikely and also economically unnecessary that all news media outlets will be neutral or nonpartisan. Thus, is seems more likely that the overall finding of no aggregate bias is created by Republican outlets being offset by Democratic outlets. Or vice versa, as one may prefer.

As an example, consider Blumberg's (1954) original study of coverage of the 1952 election. As mentioned in chapter 4, journalism professor Nathan Blumberg attempted to formally evaluate the degree to which newspaper coverage of the election displayed a preference for the Republican candidate. He examined the content of thirty-five newspapers, selected to represent the nation's newspapers both geographically and also in terms of size and prestige; he formally measured the content along twelve dimensions as well as presenting a qualitative evaluation of the tone of the copy he was reading, and reporting the editorial evaluation of the paper.

In the aggregate, Blumberg's data suggests that, far from one-sidedly favoring the Republican Dwight Eisenhower, as charged by then-out-going-President Harry Truman (Truman, 1952), the thirty-five newspapers in total were quite well balanced in their coverage. The coverage, in terms of volume, at least, broke out to 50.9 percent Democrat to 49.1 percent Republican. This small difference is not statistically significant and in formal terms the volumes of coverage are essentially identical. In their editorials the papers preferred Eisenhower 26 to 7 (with two not endorsing) but their news coverage was reasonably balanced on the whole.

Examining individual newspapers within the sample, though, shows some substantial biases. Two of the papers, both well-known and well-respected nationally (in a few years they would be named as members of the nation's Prestige Press, as mentioned in chapter 4) had 60 to 40 splits in their coverage: the *Milwaukee Journal* favored Stevenson and the *Los Angeles Times* Eisenhower (and his vice-presidential candidate, Richard Nixon).

The *Journal* and the *Los Angeles Times* were not the most egregiously biased newspapers by any means. Two-thirds of the election coverage in Colonel Rupert McCormack's *Chicago Tribune* was devoted to the Republican candidate, and over three-quarters of the coverage in the *Indianapolis Star* was of Eisenhower. On the other hand, over 70 percent of the news coverage of the *Great Falls Tribune* was of the Stevenson campaign. These are total figures measured across the entire length of campaign; in short, they are actual examples of bias as we have defined it. The newspaper industry as a whole (TV coverage of presidential campaigns was virtually negligible in those days) appears to have been balanced, at least to the ability of Blumberg's methods to examine it, but it is clear that there were individual news media outlets that were biased in their coverage.

In order to create a more complete picture of media bias in presidential elections, it might be worthwhile to examine the behavior of individual news media outlets. We know, from chapter 2, that news media outlets are not simple organizations with unitary goals. They are, instead, complex entities that have multiple essential natures, any or all of which may potentially manifest themselves in their news reports. A variety of scholars have proposed ways that at least some of the different natures of a news media outlet may influence its coverage of political campaigns, and the database accumulated for this study will enable us to test some of these theories.

NEWS MEDIA OUTLETS AS PROPERTY

The question of the role of ownership in influencing the content of coverage of issues by news media outlets lies at the heart of the fundamental disagreement about bias in the media. Conservatives (e.g. Bozell & Baker, 1990; Dautrich & Hartley, 1999) routinely point to opinion polls taken of news reporters that demonstrate that they typically support Democratic candidates to a large degree. Depending on the person making the point, this is taken as evidence that reporters will either deliberately or subconsciously bias the content of their reports to favor the side they prefer.

For people who believe that media news outlets are consistently conservative in perspective, the critical element influencing news content is not the political identity of the reporter, but instead the politics of the owner/publisher. As the media observer/critic A. J. Liebling (1961/1975) put it, "Freedom of the press is guaranteed only to those who own one" (p. 32). Owners are presumed to be essentially conservative in politics, as they belong, in broad terms, to demographic classifications associated with conservatism: older, higher in economic status and associated with business interests. In addition, for many years the editorial positions of a great many newspapers supported Republican candidates. For instance, in 1952, 82 percent of endorsing papers preferred Eisenhower over Stevenson on their editorial pages (*Editor & Publisher*, 1992). Routinely, editorials have supported Republican candidates (Bagdikian, 1972); the editorial preference favoring Clinton in 1992 was only the second time in the post–World War II period that a majority of papers supported a Democratic candidate editorially (Garbeau, 1992).

This debate, of course, is engendered in part by the focus on considering different natural aspects of news media outlets. The conservative position is considering outlets as journalistic entities, produced and staffed by journalists who are regarded as broadly liberal in worldview. This position entirely neglects the ethical aspects of the journalistic profession, and that journalists are trained and expected to keep their personal opinions out of their reporting. Instead, it assumes that, either deliberately or subconsciously, reporters will bias their coverage to conform to their prejudices, and further, that there are no institutional checks on this behavior.

The liberal position takes the perspective that news media outlets are property, owned by people who are willing to use their economic power to influence the content being produced to serve their personal, presumably conservative, interests. It, too, is oversimplified even if one takes into account that it is neglecting all the other natures of a news media outlet, as discussed in chapter 2. It presupposes, for instance, that all, or a large proportion of, owners are conservative in political beliefs, when it is known that prominent journalistic families, for instance, the Grahams, and the Ochs and Sulzberg-ers, tend to have preferences for moderate to liberal policies, and that other owners might place questions of profit ahead of questions of politics.

Inherently, though, this disagreement between liberal and conservative critics is ultimately about the locus of control in the news media outlet. If the conservative thesis is correct, the beliefs of reporters control the ideology of news reports; if the liberal position is correct, control must lie with manage-ment/ownership.

Importantly, these positions each imply testable hypotheses about the na-ture and valence of reporting in a given news media outlet. First, it is known that, regardless of their impact on news reporting, which is yet to be seen, owners and publishers play a very large, if not absolute, role in the determina-tion of the endorsement policy of an individual newspaper. In fact, the choice of which candidate to endorse in a presidential election is one of the few editorial policies that owners specifically reserve to themselves (St. Dizier, 1985; see also Chinlund, 2004), and bitter debates between the publisher and the day-to-day editors and staff of a newspaper continue to take place dur-ing virtually every campaign to this day (c.f. *Washington Post*, 1984; Rosen, 2004). So it can be presumed that, to the extent possible, the opinions of management on a given campaign are indicated by the newspaper's editorial endorsement. If management possesses and routinely uses the ability to influ-ence news coverage of the campaign to advance their own goals, then it is reasonable to assume that they will do so to favor their preferred candidate, and therefore there will be an association between the candidate endorsed and the candidate favored in coverage. Indeed, this was uncovered in a previous, although less advanced, study (D'Alessio & Allen, 2006).

Contrariwise, if the beliefs of conservative critics are correct and that re-porters who are liberal influence a news media outlet's campaign coverage in a liberal direction, we should observe two things. First, there will be no relationship between the outlet's coverage and its endorsement. Under the operation of this model of media behavior, while reporters may influence the coverage to suit their preferences, they do not make or control the editorial endorsements, which are the purviews of publishers and owners. Being created by distinct entities with unrelated goals, therefore, there is no necessary relationship between coverage and endorsement in this model. Also, if this model is true, if reporters are liberal and consequently show favoritism to Democratic candidates and are in control of the news coverage, then there should be a preponderance of outlets whose coverage favors the Democrat (that is, with positive values of d'). It should be noted immediately that this is not consistent with the findings reported in chapter 4. (It is difficult to describe a small, if statistically significant, difference in the valence of coverage alone among content elements, as a "preponderance.")

In order to test the validity of these competing models, we used the studies in our database to examine the relationship between the attitudes of management and biases in presidential election coverage. This particular test is limited to newspapers, as the TV networks and the big three newsmagazines (*Time, Newsweek,* and *US News and World Report*) do not routinely endorse candidates; while it might be possible to make guesses about their editorial preferences, it is not possible within the scope of this study to determine them absolutely.

From the database we located all the studies that reported content coverage characteristics for individual newspapers. The characteristics that we looked at were: the number of articles on either (Republican or Democratic) campaign; the amount of coverage of either campaign (typically measured in column inches); the number of photographs of either candidate; and the aggregate size of photographs (also typically measured in column inches). This was done for all three sorts of bias: volume, valence, and selection.

We then attempted to determine the endorsement made by each individual newspaper. Occasionally this would be reported by the original study but in many cases it was necessary to consult the lists of newspaper endorsements published in *Editor & Publisher* until 1996, and subsequently compiled on *Wikipedia.* Newspapers were excluded from this study if they made (or reported) no endorsement or endorsed third party candidates, or if their coverage was absolutely balanced ($d' = 0.00$).

We then constructed contingency tables matching the newspapers' coverage, Democratic or Republican, to their endorsements, Democratic or Republican. We further broke this data down based on two additional factors. First, we separated the Prestige Press newspapers from the non-Prestige papers. This was done because the research program of Stempel and his associates have led to the Prestige Press being overrepresented in our sample of newspapers, as was pointed out in chapter 4. Further, it seems not unreasonable to conclude that one way a member of the Prestige Press gets to be identified as a "prestigious" newspaper is because there is a different relationship between management and the working reporters than there is at other papers. The nature of the difference is not particularly relevant; what is important is that a difference in relationship between publishers and reporters would be manifest in the relationship between editorial endorsement and coverage.

Second, we broke the data between the 1972 and 1976 elections. One reason for this is that breaking the data represents a surrogate for time as a variable; there are too few measurements of many of the elections for us to consider the data on an election-by-election basis, but there are systematic changes in the newspaper industry over time that may influence the results. For instance, in the time period covered by this study, the number of newspapers operating in the United States declines (Straubhaar & LaRose, 2006), the number that are publicly owned increases (see below) and the number choosing not to endorse any candidate at all increases (Giobbe, 1996), all of these trends proceeding more or less steadily. Any of these might potentially influence the relationship between endorsement and coverage. The other reason for breaking the data is that commentators and observers (see Pournelle, 1992, for example) have pointed out that the proceedings of the Watergate scandal, occurring between the 1972 and 1976 election campaigns, created changes both in the relationship between the press and the presidency, and also the laws regarding campaigning, which also might influence the outcome of the study.

Once the data are collected, they can be aggregated into contingency tables that cross-reference the valence of endorsement with the valence of coverage; that is, we can count the number of Democratic-endorsing papers and separate them by the number whose coverage favors the Democrat and the number favoring the Republican, and then the same for the Republican-endorsing papers. The resulting contingency table can be tested using the χ^2 test statistic (with one degree of freedom), where a significant χ^2 would indicate an association between valence of endorsement and valence of coverage, and a nonsignificant test would be evidence of a lack of relationship between endorsements and coverage.

The results are presented in table 5.1, both the distribution of papers by coverage and endorsement and also the χ^2 test statistics. Stated simply, the results show that on the whole there is overall a strong relationship between the paper's endorsement and the valence of its coverage: Republican-endorsing papers are more likely to provide their readers with coverage favoring the Republican candidate and the campaign coverage in Democratic-endorsing papers is more likely to favor the Democrat. Coverage and endorsement

Table 5.1.   Coverage vs. endorsements in newspapers

			R-R	D-D	R-D	D-R	χ^2	p
Overall			148	123	81	80	27.4	<.001
	Prestige Press		49	90	40	54	7.0	<.01
		'72 and earlier	42	58	29	5	38.3	<.001
		'76 and later	7	32	11	49	2.8	n.s.
	Non-Prestige Papers		99	33	41	26	12.1	<.001
		'72 and earlier	71	18	21	2	32.4	<.001
		'76 and later	28	15	20	24	1.0	n.s.

Note: R is Republican and D is Democrat. In each pair the first letter refers to endorsement and the second to coverage. All χ^2 are at 1 degree of freedom.

agreed in 63 percent of cases, almost two-thirds of the time. This is statistically significant and consistent with earlier findings in this area (D'Alessio & Allen, 2006).

Examining the breakdowns by date, however, indicate that this relationship has essentially disappeared since the mid-1970s. While endorsement and coverage agreed over three-quarters of the time (76.8 percent) for the elections prior to 1976, within the group of studies examining the elections of 1976 and later there is essentially no relationship between a paper's endorsement and its coverage, at least so far as the group of newspapers represented in the sample is concerned. Endorsements and coverage for the later time period agree less than half the time (44 percent), but the nonsignificant χ^2 tests indicated that they too should be taken as essentially unrelated.

The obvious conclusion to be made from these results is that it used to be true that owners and publishers would set the tone of coverage provided by their papers; however, this effect has essentially disappeared as a general tendency. While it is still possible that individual newspaper publishers may still choose to intervene in the political coverage in their papers—in fact the specific case of J. Mellon Scaife and the *Pittsburgh Tribune-Review* (Lieberman, 2000) is discussed in chapter 2—this appears to be an idiosyncratic rather than general practice in recent years.

It should also be noted that in the period of 1976 and later, coverage of 108 of the papers in the study favored the Republican candidates and 78 the Democratic candidates.

What this combination of results tells us is that claims by conservatives that liberal journalists bias the news as a whole in favor of the candidates they personally prefer is incorrect. First, to the extent that there is systematic control of the content, it is exercised by management, not by reporters. And second, the presumption that a lack of management control would lead to a liberal (pro-Democratic) bias is unsupported by the data.

Finally, the data clearly show that these findings apply more or less equally to the Prestige Papers and the remainder. Although the influence of management is somewhat stronger in the non-Prestige outlets, the fact is that both sets of papers show the same pattern of results: a strong association between endorsement and coverage prior to the 1976 election, and the two unrelated in the elections of 1976 and later.

Additional clarity on this finding may be gained by considering a single individual example. In the case of at least one of the newspapers repeatedly examined across the course of time represented by this research, ownership and workers are essentially the same group of people. Specifically, as we have already seen, majority control of the *Milwaukee Journal* (now the *Journal-Sentinal*) is cooperatively held by the *Journal*'s employees. As described in chapter 2, people working for the *Journal* are afforded the opportunity to buy shares in the paper entitling them to a share of the profits, and must yield them back to the paper if they leave it.

Under these conditions, as the ownership and the reporters are essentially the same group, at the *Journal* it should be possible to observe the action of the biases of reporters (if any) uncontrolled by the preferences of management. If it were true that reporters (who are conceded to generally hold liberal beliefs) allow their beliefs to "color" their writing, then we should most clearly observe this in the reporting that takes place in the *Journal*.

There are twelve measurements of volumetric bias in the *Journal* and only one of valenced bias. The twelve measures of volumetric bias yield an average d' of .059 ($p < .05$), indicating a small, pro-Democratic bias. How small? A d' of 0.59 is a bias of less than 53 percent Democratic coverage to 47 percent Republican. This is, however, statistically significant, and does support the contention that reporters as a class favor the Democrats over the Republicans in the absence of management control. On the other hand, the degree of that favoritism is almost certainly insubstantial. It is certainly substantially less than the degree to which reporters favor liberal positions (typical studies suggest that, if it was measured using the d' statistic, the preference of reporters for liberal positions and candidates would yield d's in excess of the .15 to .2 to range, as seen in chapter 2). This may mean that reporters are indeed prejudiced toward liberal positions and may not entirely succeed at moderating their beliefs in their writings despite their ethical training and requirements. Or it may be indicative of any of a thousand other things, such as content in the *Journal* reflecting the working-class, pro-labor nature of the community it serves. It is certainly not a large bias.

The one measure of valence bias was negative in sign ($d' = -.034$). No conclusions can or should be drawn from that.

On the whole the data from the *Journal* cannot contradict the overall conclusions; data on one newspaper is generally inferior to data from numerous newspapers. But if the attitudes of reporters are in the $d' = .2$ range and their behavior is closer to the $d' = .06$ range, it is reasonable to conclude that reporters are deliberately attempting to avoid allowing their attitudes to bias their reporting, and largely succeeding.

PUBLIC VS. PRIVATE OWNERSHIP

A second area of debate is also related to the question of ownership, but in this case the tension between the concept of a news media outlet as property, to be dealt with as the owner wills and subject to the owner's whims, and the concept of a news media outlet as a commercial entity, which is subject in principle to the "invisible hand" of the marketplace and therefore needs to be sufficiently responsive to its audience's sensibilities so as to not offend them.

As we discussed in chapter 2, all news media outlets have some kind of tension between these two states, unless the outlet in question is owned and run solely for profit. Yet, it is unlikely that a news media outlet is run solely for profit: news media outlets are generally not regarded as excellent investments and often the money invested in them does not return at the same rate that it would invested in other businesses (c.f. Buffett, 2009). More commonly, at least anecdotally, people purchase or start news media outlets, particularly newspapers, in part for the political clout that they possess, including the examples cited in chapter 2. Of course, television stations are a separate question as an investment property, but in the case of television we are also talking about the network news, which is rarely under the control of the owner of an affiliated station.

The tension between profit and ideology becomes a particular concern when the news media outlet in question is part of an entity that is publicly owned, rather than privately. A privately owned business has an element of freedom vis-á-vis its profitability: the owners can choose to forgo some of their profits (if any) in order to satisfy their whims with regard to controlling content and policy (*see* Shoemaker & Reese, 1996).

On the other hand, a publicly owned company is expected to be responsive to the needs of its shareholders. To become a publicly held company, the company offers shares in the ownership of the company for sale to the public. The purchase price of the shares is to be reinvested in the business, allowing it to expand. In return, however, the company is expected to give the shareholders some form of financial return on their investment in the business, either in the form of dividends paid from the company's revenues or in terms of increasing the value of the shares by creating business growth, or some combination of the two (Gartner & Gartner, 1998).

From the standpoint of a publicly owned news media outlet, the expectation that that the shareholders of the company should receive a return on their investment is expected to place some form of restriction on the outlet's political behavior, specifically, to moderate its political views. While a privately owned news media outlet can be as extreme politically as its owner pleases, as it is the owner's purse that is affected if the outlet's politics causes it to lose users, publicly owned news media outlets are expected to maximize returns on the public's investment by placing profit ahead of politics. In this case, they are expected to display moderate political views, since the middle, or moderate, path is by definition where the bulk of the users lie politically. (This presupposes that political views are distributed normally, along a "bell-curve" distribution. Under the bell curve, most of the people are in the middle, not out at the extremes.)

The question of public versus private ownership has been examined empirically by Wang (2003), who compared the differences in coverage of the 2000 presidential campaign between the *Boston Globe*, a publicly owned newspaper, and the *Boston Herald*, which was at that time privately held. Wang's results showed that the coverage in each favored the Republican, but as he predicted, the *Herald*'s coverage was significantly and substantially more favorable to the Republican than the *Globe*'s. Although not specifically considering the matter of ownership, Kenney and Simpson (1993) performed much the same analysis comparing the coverage of the 1992 campaign in the *Washington Post* to that of the *Washington Times*, and again founded that the privately owned *Times*' coverage was more extremely partisan than that in the publicly owned *Post*.

This cannot be taken as proof, however. As one might expect, coverage by two newspapers each of two elections is not the kind of evidence on which to base general statements. In addition, there are other differences between the papers besides their type of ownership. The *Herald* and the *Times* endorsed the Republican and the *Globe* the Democrat while the *Post* does not make endorsements for president, for instance, and the *Globe* and the *Post* have substantially higher circulations than their competitors. We do not know if any of these differences matter, but for the purposes of drawing conclusions we must recognize that these represent uncontrolled differences that might have caused the results Wang, and Kenney and Simpson, observed.

To consider the influence of type of ownership (public or private) we returned to the database of newspapers and their coverage constructed to look at the impact of ownership above, and added to it information about the type of ownership, public or private, of the paper in every case where we were able to ascertain it, which we were in 262 of 266 cases. (Recall that in many cases it was possible to make multiple measurements from the same newspaper's coverage.) Basically, previous to the 1968 election all the papers in the sample were privately owned or owned by consortia not open to the membership of the general public. The first major paper to offer ownership shares publicly was *The New York Times*, in 1967, but increasingly since then newspaper or media conglomerates have been going public or been purchased by publicly owned companies such as Disney or News Corp (Straubhaar & LaRose, 2006).

We excluded television network news from this analysis, as the television networks have been publicly owned essentially from their inception, and certainly during the time period that we have data on them from (1968 to the present). Thus there are no privately owned networks to compare them to.

Newsmagazines, on the other hand, can also be studied in this regard. Of the big three, one, *Time*, has been publicly owned since the 1940s, while *US News and World Report* has been and is still privately owned. *Newsweek* was the property of the Washington Post Company until 2010, and thus for the purposes of this study was publicly owned with the rest of the company starting in 1971. Thus, in examining the impact of newsmagazine ownership on news coverage, we can compare *Time* and *Newsweek* to *US News and World Report* (since the first study of newsmagazine content we located was conducted after 1971).

Logically, to recast the expectations of the impact of the type of ownership into the terms we have been using, the implication is that publicly owned papers will be more moderate in their reporting than privately owned papers, which is to say that the average d' for the publicly owned papers will be closer to zero—whether positive or negative in sign—than the average privately owned paper. This does not appear to related to partisan bias in reporting until one recalls, from above, that there are more Republican papers than Democratic ones. If there is also a preponderance of Republican papers among those that are privately owned, it could be that the greater extremity in coverage expected in private papers would not be offset between parties, creating a de facto bias.

To test this, we took the absolute, that is, un-signed, value of d' for each newspaper's and newsmagazine's coverage of each campaign, measured along the following dimensions: volumetric biases in the number of stories and amount of space accorded each party; the number and size of photographs; also valence measures of the text of the coverage. We broke the values down by whether the paper or magazine in question was publicly or privately owned, and then compared the average amount of unbalance between them using the same d' statistic.

Table 5.2a.   Influence of private vs. public ownership on coverage

	Ownership	d′	sd	n	t	p
Absolute values						
All newspapers	Private	.161	.182	454	0.55	n.s.
	Public	.154	.133	195		
Prestige Press	Private	.114	.122	227	0.57	n.s.
	Public	.107	.087	90		
Changers	Private	.136	.131	144	0.89	n.s.
	Public	.123	.105	118		
All newsmagazines	Private	.141	.110	11	0.44	n.s.
	Public	.125	.067	22		
Signed valences						
All newspapers	Private	−.054	.237	454	0.11	n.s.
	Public	−.052	.197	195		
Prestige Press	Private	−.023	.165	227	0.28	n.s.
	Public	−.028	.135	90		
Changers	Private	−.050	.182	144	1.29	n.s.
	Public	−.023	.160	118		
All newsmagazines	Private	−.097	.154	11	1.04	n.s.
	Public	−.040	.138	22		

Because of the wide variety of studies that make up this report, we also looked at two major subsets of newspapers, the first being the Prestige Press papers, as they have been studied repeatedly across time, and the second being the papers on which we had measurements on both before they were taken public and again afterwards. (These are termed "changers" and include the *Baltimore Sun, Boston Globe, Burlington Free Press, Chicago Tribune, Dallas Morning News, Detroit Free Press, Detroit News, Hartford Courant, Kansas City Star, Los Angeles Times, Louisville Courier-Journal, Miami Herald, The New York Times, Philadelphia Inquirer, Sioux Falls Argus Leader* and the *Washington Post.*) We felt that if a change from private to public ownership was to have a moderating effect on a newspaper's election campaign coverage, it would be most obvious in the group of changers, since they act as their own control group for purposes of comparison.

Since newsmagazines are not members of the Prestige Press and none of them changed ownership status within the time frame we could study, this breakdown into subgroups was not conducted for newsmagazines.

The results are presented at the top of table 5.2a, under the heading of "Absolute values." Please note that in this case a positive *d′* is not indicative of a pro-Democrat bias; it is merely the average size of a bias, whether for the Democrats or the Republicans. Differences in *d′* between publicly and privately owned papers was tested using the Student's *t* test statistic (Lin, 1976).

In all four cases (all newspapers, Prestige Press, changers, and all news-magazines), the aggregated unbalances across the privately owned newspapers is larger than that across publicly owned newspapers. However, none of these differences is statistically significant, which is to say that statistically speaking, each of the measured differences is indistinguishable from no difference at all. To put the observed results into context, the largest difference in unbalance of coverage is between the publicly owned newsmagazines (*Time* and *Newsweek*; d' = .125) and the privately owned *US News and World Report* (d' = .141). The difference between the two groups (d' = .016) is equivalent in magnitude to a difference of 50.8 percent on one side of a question to 49.2 percent on the other.

In the social sciences, results of "no difference" are always treated carefully, as the logic of statistical testing is based on the idea of "no difference" being a starting point that must be rejected by a fairly substantial amount of proof; in short, statistical tests favor a finding of no difference between groups. To be certain that we were not overlooking any particular phenomenon, we conducted the same test again, this time retaining the sign of the original d' for each given newspaper's and newsmagazine's coverage. We did this to see if there was a generalized trend of newspapers moving in policy from only one extreme (either pro-Democrat or pro-Republican) toward the middle as their ownership changes from private to public (as opposed to moving toward the middle from the extremes on either side, as was the premise of the previous test).

These results are at the bottom of table 5.2a, under the heading "Signed valences." Again, there are no significant differences in coverage attributable to the type of ownership.

In a final attempt to detect any differences in coverage between privately owned and publicly owned newspapers, we further subdivided the two groups by whether they had made an endorsement of a presidential candidate during the campaign they were covering, yielding a four-way breakdown of papers into the categories of "Privately owned/Endorsing," "Publicly owned/Endorsing," "Privately owned/Non-endorsing," and "Publicly owned/Non-endorsing," and again aggregated each group by the absolute value of each paper's coverage imbalance. Our intention in doing this was to distinguish papers that were, for lack of a better term, engaged politically in the election from those that were not, the expectation being that engaged newspapers, as represented by papers having made an editorial endorsement for one of the candidates, should have greater internal motivations to engage in biased coverage than disengaged newspapers. Newsmagazines were omitted from this analysis as they do not endorse candidates.

These results are presented in table 5.2b. First, while the gap in unbalance of coverage between privately and publicly owned papers is larger for papers endorsing presidential candidates than for non-endorsing papers, the differences between public and private outlets are not statistically significant for either the endorsers ($t = 0.96$) or non-endorsers ($t = .078$). In short, the difference in coverage between publicly owned and privately owned newspaper is again essentially zero to the extent of our ability to measure it. Therefore, we have to conclude that the nature of ownership has no discernable effect on the magnitude of bias in news coverage of presidential election campaigns on the whole. While there are individual counter examples, the results here suggest that they occur so infrequently as to have no measurable impact on the industry as a whole.

In retrospect, while the logic that predicts that there should be differences in coverage between news media outlets with different types of ownership, with publicly owned outlets driven toward the political middle in search of large, profitable audiences is compelling, this logic probably does not take into account the mechanisms by which news media outlets move from being private property to being publicly owned (and, less frequently, the reverse) or change ideology. In essence, there are two common pathways to private news media outlets becoming publicly owned. One is for the outlet's existing management to choose to incorporate and sell shares. While this in principle moves the paper from the control of the original management to that of the shareholders, in reality this generally leaves the current management in place to continue doing as they have always done, as the influence of shareholders is diffuse and indirect (and functions through the mechanism of shareholders voting for the board of directors and/or "voting with their feet" by selling the stock, driving the price down). In fact, the retention of editorial control by the current management is formalized in a number of corporations, as we have seen in the example of The New York Times Company, in which there are two different types of stock issued, one associated with managerial control that is retained by the owners, and a second that operates strictly as an investment vehicle.

Table 5.2b. Public vs. private ownership, endorsing vs. non-endorsing newspapers

		d'	sd	n	t	p
Endorsing papers						
	Private	.154	.163	326	0.96	n.s.
	Public	.140	.120	110		
Non-endorsing papers						
	Private	.179	.221	135	0.78	n.s.
	Public	.177	.151	79		

The second mechanism by which a news media outlet changes between public and private ownership is for the outlet to be purchased by a larger entity with a different ownership status, for instance, as when the *Kansas City Star* was purchased by Disney. In this case, however, it seems likely that the outlet is being purchased because it is seen by the corporation as being a potential source of profit *as it already is*. Being purchased can involve any number of changes, including layoffs and/or the restructuring of the budget, but in general these changes do not necessarily include an explicit change in ideology. Frankly, if a new corporate owner radically restructures the ideology of a going concern, it risks destroying whatever value that existed in the outlet in the first place by alienating whatever current user base the outlet is currently reaching. If a corporation wants a newspaper that expresses a specific ideological bias, it is probably simpler and financially more efficient to simply start a new paper—as was the case with the *Washington Times*—than to buy an existing paper and change its politics.

And, of course, we have seen one example of a newspaper deliberately changing its ideological position, that being the *Los Angeles Times* in the early 1960s (see chapter 1). In that particular instance, the change was unrelated to ownership status: the *Times* was privately owned before the change and still privately owned for more than a decade after. The ideological shift was probably simplified by the fact that the publisher making the change was also effectively the owner. But the fact, that as it happened, the *Times* moved from the right to the middle does not imply that that is a general trend, and the data here suggests that it is not.

Of interest still would be the ideology of outlets that move from public to private ownership, which has happened in instances but is not represented in the data. For instance, billionaire Sam Zell bought the Tribune Company, parent of both the *Los Angeles Times* and *Chicago Tribune*, among others, and removed shares of the company from over-the-counter sales at the New York Stock Exchange in 2007 (Ahrens, 2007). Unfortunately, there has not been any examination of the campaign coverage of the *Times* or *Tribune* (or any of the Times-Mirror papers) for the 2008 election yet. It is still possible that a difference between public and private ownership could be found in that case (as, if you take a newspaper private, its nature as property is emphasized), but the data we need to test that possibility currently do not exist.

THE PRO- (ANTI-?) INCUMBENCY BIAS

Another area in which media have been expected to show preferences for or against certain candidates is in dealing with electoral incumbents. As with many of the questions we have been examining, there are two major schools of thought on this question as well.

As has been noted routinely, part of the business nature of a news media outlet is that the "news hole" has to be filled every day. From a financial standpoint, it is the news that attracts users to the advertisements, and the advertisements that pay for the news operations. As part of the process of newsgathering, reporters develop contacts and relationships with elected officials and their staffs, which in turn facilitates newsgathering efforts. In consequence, the reasoning goes, incumbent elected officials have greater representation in the news pages (since news about them is easier to gather), leading in turn to an inadvertent pro-incumbency bias.

Additionally, Stovall (1984) has compiled a list of three critical advantages a sitting president enjoys in campaigning for reelection that are relevant to this discussion. First, the president *is* the president, and a campaigning president has access to whatever respect and prestige accrues to the office of president. For instance, a sitting president is addressed with the title of "President," which is generally uncommon for challengers (Theodore Roosevelt and Grover Cleveland being notable exceptions). Second, a sitting president has a degree of control over newsworthy events external to the campaign, by presenting or vetoing legislation, or engaging in foreign policy, or otherwise performing the duties of the office of president. The 2008 election season, for instance, featured a number of newsworthy attempts on the joint part of the executive and legislative branches to alleviate the effects of the recession the nation was currently undergoing, attempts that challengers could not be party to except as critics. The choice to make these attempts was made by people whose parties would be participating in the campaign and consequently there was the opportunity for them to benefit from the news coverage of these attempts. And third, as president, a candidate for reelection has greater access to media simply because some of his or her actions are newsworthy. (It is worth noting that Stovall found no advantage to incumbency in his research, although he attributed this to the peculiarities of the 1980 campaign, which he was studying.)

At the same time, other scholars (e.g. Lowry & Shidler, 1998; Graber, 1997) point out that the political nature of news media outlets could reasonably be expected to lead to an anti-incumbent bias. Part of the role of news media is supposed to be to act as a watchdog on, or adversary to, the party in power, to challenge the government as part of the media's political role as the representative of the voters, as discussed in chapter 2. Such challenges, while they may or may not affect the volume of coverage that an incumbent receives, clearly imply that the tone of coverage of incumbents could be expected to be negative, as critical responses tend to be negative in tone. This in turn could potentially lead to a bias in the valence in coverage against the incumbent. It should be noted, however, that Lowry and Shidler (1998) report finding little or no support for an anti-incumbent effect in coverage of the 1992 campaign.

As with the question of public versus private ownership, there is nothing inherently partisan about pro- or anti-incumbency biases. However, during the time frame encompassed by this research (1948–2008) there have been six Republican incumbent presidents (Eisenhower, Nixon, Ford, Reagan, George H. W. Bush and George W. Bush) and only four Democratic incumbents (Truman, Johnson, Carter and Clinton). Equally sized incumbency-related biases during the reporting of each election campaign would therefore mathematically lead to the appearance of a net bias toward Republican party. That is, a pro-incumbency bias would yield a pro-Republican bias across all the studies we have considered herein simply because there have been more Republican incumbents. Obviously, the reverse could be true: an anti-incumbency bias would by the same reasoning be associated with a pro-Democratic bias.

Additionally, the database we have accumulated here allows us to make more thorough tests of the incumbency and anti-incumbency biases. Neither of the studies mentioned above (Stovall, 1984; Lowry & Shidler, 1998) found any effect either pro or con, but each considered only one campaign and coverage by only a small number of news media outlets. In our database, we have examinations of newspaper coverage of all the campaigns listed above, and of television coverage of seven of them. This would allow us to draw more general conclusions than previous researchers could.

To examine this question of incumbency biases, we returned to the master analysis table used to consider the overall question of aggregate media bias used in chapter 4 (see Appendix A). We extracted from it the studies of election campaigns that involved incumbents (1948, 1956, 1964, 1972, 1976, 1980, 1984, 1992, 1996 and 2004) and recoded the results from a scale where positive d's are associated with Democratic candidates to a scale where positive d's are associated with incumbents. We then aggregated the results of these studies as described in chapter 3.

The aggregate of all results across all studies involving incumbents yielded what amounted to no incumbency effect at all in either direction, a d' of .013, which did not differ statistically or substantively from zero, indicating no difference between coverage of incumbents or challengers.

As we have pointed out earlier, negative results are generally regarded as suspect because statistical tests are designed to set the bar relatively high in terms of accepting small effects as "real." Also, it should be noted, as we did for the aggregate of "bias in the media" for chapter 4, this is an "apples and oranges" omnibus test that treats all media and types of bias as the same.

Table 5.3.   Effect sizes for incumbency effects

				d'	sd	n	t	p
Overall				.013	.142	116	0.99	n.s.
	Newspapers			.023	.121	51	1.36	n.s.
		Volume		.047	.127	33	2.13	<.05
			Republican	.106	.126	17	3.45	<.001
			Democrat	−.014	.097	16	0.58	n.s.
		Valence		−.060	.094	16	2.55	<.05
			Republican	−.071	.075	12	3.28	<.005
			Democrat	−.035	.422	4	0.17	n.s.
	Television			−.044	.159	54	2.03	<.05
		Volume		−.007	.140	27	0.26	n.s.
			Republican	−.015	.140	22	0.50	n.s.
			Democrat	.026	.134	5	0.43	n.s.
		Valence		−.077	.178	27	2.24	<.05
			Republican	−.111	.195	20	2.55	<.01
			Democrat	.028	.108	7	0.69	n.s.

Notes: 11 studies of media other than newspapers or television are included in the overall test. Two tests of selection bias are included in the newspaper total.

More importantly, the discussion above suggests that while pro-incumbency biases might lie in the volume of coverage (because incumbents are expected to have greater access to the news hole), anti-incumbency effects would lie in the valence of coverage (as a consequence of the news media's role as critic), leading to the possibility that the result observed above is a consequence of biases in one area being offset in the aggregate by biases in the other. Thus, we conducted a second test, breaking measures of volume from the measures of valence. We also separated newspapers from television, in that in terms of covering presidential campaigns the roles of the two are very different, specifically that newspapers must report on behalf of local audiences while the television networks' news reports are explicitly intended for a national audience. Additionally, the relatively small number of network news reporters can generally demand higher levels of access from incumbent presidents than the larger number of reporters from individual newspapers, each of which has a much smaller user base than any of the television newscasts.

All the breakdowns are also presented in table 5.3. For newspapers there is no overall net incumbency bias, either pro or con (d' = .023). Television coverage shows a statistically significant anti-incumbent bias on the other hand (d' = −.044), although it is fairly small (47.8 percent coverage favoring the incumbent to 52.2 percent for the challenger).

However, when delving into the different types of bias, a separate picture of treatment of incumbents emerges. For newspaper coverage of presidential campaigns, there is an overall, statistically significant (albeit not large, $d' = .047$) pro-incumbent bias in the volume of coverage, but simultaneously a significant anti-incumbency bias ($d' = -.060$) in the valence of coverage. In short, there was more newspaper coverage of incumbents, but the coverage of the incumbents was also more negative in tone. In other words, both models are supported to a degree: incumbents get more coverage, and coverage that is more critical.

Television news coverage was balanced in volume, but also showed an anti-incumbent bias in valence ($d' = -.077$) similar in magnitude to the anti-incumbency bias found in the newspapers.

Once we observed a positive (pro-incumbent) bias in volume for newspapers and an anti-incumbent bias in valence (tone) for both newspapers and television, the final question we wanted to consider was whether there were partisan differences associated with them. To accomplish this, we further broke the studies of volume and valence of coverage in both newspapers and television down by party. As we see on table 5.3, the incumbency biases, pro- and con-, seem only to affect Republicans. Republican candidates get significantly more coverage in newspapers than their challengers ($d' = .106$ for Republican incumbents, $-.014$ for Democrats); the coverage they get is significantly more negative in tone ($d' = -.071$ for Republicans, $-.035$ for Democrats). Similarly, the valence of coverage of incumbent Republican incumbents on television news is negative ($d' = -.111$) while that of Democratic incumbents is neutral ($d' = .028$).

It should be noted that this is the first serious example of partisan bias we have uncovered thus far: Republican incumbents get more newspaper space than their challengers while newspapers and television news reports are critical of Republican incumbents and not Democratic incumbents. These are also the largest effects we have seen by a fairly substantial margin. The d' for the tone of coverage for Republican incumbents, $d' = -.111$, indicates that statements are 55.55 percent favorable to Democratic challengers (or unfavorable to Republican incumbents) and only 44.45 percent favorable to the Republican incumbent.

Is this difference in tone large enough to be discernable to the average voter? That is both unknown and beyond the scope of this study; it is a legitimate question, however, and worthy of being examined in the future.

INDIVIDUAL OUTLETS

The question of individual outlets and whether they persistently show favoritism to one party or another is an interesting one in that sometimes the discussion is almost at the level of so-called urban legends. Question: Why does everyone "know" that newspaper A is biased in favor of liberals or conservatives? Answer: Because everyone says it is. This constitutes almost an ad hoc use of a Delphi-like technique, wherein a group of knowledgeable persons are consulted on a general topic and their answers aggregated to arrive at what amounts to an educated "guesstimate" of the truth.

In some cases, this is merely a matter of perception. As we have seen (in chapter 3), opinions on bias are based on subjective phenomena that are sometimes unrelated to reality (Watts et al., 1999). On the other hand, sometimes a news media outlet is explicitly partisan in its reporting, and deliberately so, in order that the outlet reflect the ideology of the owner or proprietor, or as a deliberate marketing choice designed to align the outlet with a specific, well-defined market of users and advertisers. As we have seen, while we expect the most users to be found in the middle of the ideological spectrum, that does not mean that there are not viable economic strategies to be taken advantage of by catering to one end of the ideological spectrum or the other, and in fact Baron (2006) has demonstrated that it is possible for a highly biased news media outlet to make greater profits than a more centrist competitor under certain conditions.

Two outlets in particular have received a great deal of attention for their ideologies, real or imagined: *The New York Times* and the Fox News Channel. *The New York Times* is regarded by many as the flagship newspaper of the U.S. newspaper industry—when the Prestige Press was being named, *The New York Times* led the list—and as a result many scholars use coverage of an issue in the *Times* as a surrogate for newspaper coverage generally. Further, political candidates such as Robert Dole routinely conclude that the *Times* sets the agenda for all media.

This is doubly of concern to some commentators because the editorial policies of *The New York Times* are explicitly left of center (Okrent, 2004). These are the causes that the Ochs family originally bought the *Times* to champion and it is to champion these causes that the Sulzberger family retains editorial control of the paper, even though it is now in principle the property of its shareholders. It is therefore assumed that the paper's preferences editorially are reflected in the news content of the paper in the form of a persistent liberal bias. Consequently, *The New York Times* is frequently named when people ask the question "What is the most liberal newspaper in the country?" (See, for instance, answers.com, 2010; yahoo.com, 2010.)

In addition, *The New York Times* is also often regarded by scholars and others as a surrogate for the news industry as a whole as a consequence of the fact that many editors report reading the *Times*. The reasoning is therefore, "As goes the *Times*, so goes the industry," despite the fact that *The New York*

Times has been known to trail rather than lead when its role in the national news hole was empirically examined (Rogers, Dearing & Chang, 1991).

Playing the role it is perceived to in the newspaper industry, the content of *The New York Times* has been criticized numerous times in the past. For instance, Bob Dole's specific complaints about *Times*, in which he labeled the paper ". . . An arm of the Democratic National Committee," (Seelye, 1996) were explicitly tested by Jamieson (2000), and in fact found to be false. Dole received more coverage in the *Times* than his Democratic opponent (Clinton), was pictured more often and quoted more often. (Lee et al., 2004, showed that the pictures of Dole were less flattering than those of Clinton, however, and there do not seem to be any tests of the tone, or valence, of the coverage, unfortunately.)

Benoit et al. (2005) conducted a retrospective study of the manner in which *The New York Times* has covered presidential election campaigns since the 1950s, and arrived at the conclusion that across those campaigns *Times* coverage had been balanced overall in terms of volume but the valence of coverage had favored the Democrats by a measurable amount ($d' = .090$, or 54.45 percent Democratic to 44.55 percent Republican). Since the primary purpose of their study was to examine trends in the style of coverage, Benoit and his colleagues did not get more deeply into the question of balance, however.

Our data shows that, exclusive of the Benoit et al. (2005) study, which is not broken down on a campaign-by-campaign basis so far as the balance data is concerned, there have been forty-four studies of the content of *The New York Times*, thirty-seven of its volume and seven of its valence. (There were no studies of selection bias in the *Times* that we were able to find.) In the studies of volume, the coverage of the Times was balanced to within our ability to measure it ($d' = .010$, $sd = .137$, $t = 0.44$, p = n.s.). Finally, the five studies of the valence of the *Times'* coverage also showed no difference at all ($d' = .058$, $sd = .148$, $t = 1.03$, p = n.s.).

On the whole, this points up, first, the relative neutrality of *The New York Times'* coverage. It certainly does not serve as "an arm of the Democratic National Committee" by any stretch of the imagination apart from the false conclusions that arise as a consequence of the hostile media effect (see chapter 3). Neither did it favor the Republican candidates; the *Times'* coverage was almost completely balanced to the limit of our ability to measure such things. Unquestionably there are papers more liberal than the Times, at least in terms of presidential campaign coverage, starting with the *Milwaukee Journal-Sentinel*, as we saw previously. It seems more likely that the *Times'* reputation of being the most liberal newspaper has more to do with perception than performance, and again points up the disjunciton between belief and reality on the judgment of bias.

It also points up a technical matter, that being the distinction between a single formal, in-depth study and a meta-analytic report such as this one. In finding that the *Times* coverage showed a bias in valence, Benoit and his colleagues (2005) looked at samples that amounted to two weeks' worth of coverage drawn from each election from 1952 to 2000, almost half a year's worth of coverage in total. By definition, in this book we are only able to work with the studies that are available, and so obviously, with only five studies of the tone or valence of the *Times'* coverage available it is clear that reporting on a majority of the elections is not represented in that particular measurement.

At the same time, Benoit et al. used a single methodology designed specifically to test the hypotheses of interest to them. The forty-four studies our results are based on were conducted by over fifty researchers and include a wider variety of possible ways of measuring bias.

In the end, both Benoit et al. and this study agree that there is no difference in the amount of space *The New York Times* devotes to Republican candidates as opposed to Democratic candidates. This is an example of balanced coverage by any definition.

Benoit and colleagues found a pro-Democrat bias in the valence of coverage whereas we did not. Given the methodological differences between our study and theirs, I would have to conclude that they are probably closer to the truth than we are on the question of valence of coverage. Certainly the data on which they base their claims on the historical valence of the *Times'* coverage is better than ours. But even if we accept Benoit et al.'s findings as superior to our own, the magnitude of the bias in tone is less than a 55 to 45 split, certainly inconsistent with being "the most liberal newspaper in the country." Recall that there were splits of 60 to 40 and larger mentioned earlier.

A second news media outlet that routinely evokes concern as to its objectivity in coverage is the Fox News channel. The editorial prejudices of Fox News are apparent and can be summarized by comparing the number of Republican political candidates who have been contributors to the channel (many, including Buchanan, Forbes, Huckabee and Palin) to the number of Democrats (none). However, as with *The New York Times* and also consistent with the rest of this report, we are explicitly not concerned with editorial content that is clearly portrayed as such, but in the content of the news reporting.

As a relatively recent creation in comparison to the broadcast television networks, Fox News is also interesting because it has no identity as a broadcast outlet and is an entity developed to fill the needs of cable TV systems. Thus it has had no history with nor threat from the restrictions on political content placed on the broadcast networks such as the Fairness Doctrine or the Equal Time Provision. Until they were deemed unconstitutional, even after they were lifted as part of the Reagan administration's general policy of deregulation of industries (Straubhaar & LaRose, 2006), it was not uncommon for Congress to threaten to reinstate them if broadcasters were found—by Congress—to be egregiously taking advantage of what was seen to be an oligopolistic control of televised news.

The threat of the Equal Time Provision (in particular) on TV network news and the lack of such in cable news implies that the political roles of broadcast networks and cable stations could potentially be quite different. As part of the broadcast continuum, for instance, the TV networks dominated the television industry before the proliferation of cable, and were routinely expected to program in the public interest. On the other hand, Fox News is situated in an environment of dozens or even hundreds of channels of competing content, an environment that empowers the economic advantages of narrowcasting to specific, well-defined audiences that could reasonably include audiences defined by ideology. Therefore, it could be instructive to look at whether the balance in news coverage for broadcast networks and cable news channels, particularly Fox News, is similar on a channel-by-channel basis.

To do this, we returned to the main database of studies listed in Appendix A and selected those that made some measurement of the content of television coverage of one or more presidential election campaigns, and presented the data broken down by network or cable channel. We located a total of forty-three measurements of either the volume or valence of CBS's network news coverage, and thirty-five each of NBC and ABC. (As with *The New York Times*, scholars who have chosen only one network to serve as a surrogate for all three have chosen CBS due to the high reputation of its news department, c.f. Stevenson, et al., 1973.) We broke those data down further by network and whether the measure under examination was one of volume or valence, so were able to estimate volumetric and valence bias in the presidential campaign coverage in each of the three networks' newscasts.

In addition, we found sixteen measurements of various other cable (Fox News, CNN, MSNBC) and broadcast (PBS) news media outlets. There were only three measurements of CNN and MSNBC and one of PBS, which is an insufficient number from which to draw any larger conclusions; however, there were nine measurements of Fox News's news productions (as opposed to their commentary). These were also broken down by type of bias, volume or valence, as was the data for the broadcast networks.

In table 5.4 we show the biases at the campaign coverage of TV network news, plus Fox News broken down by network, and once again measured using d'. Recall (from chapter 4) that there is a small, statistically significant pro-Democratic bias in the valence of television network news reporting, but none in the volume. We see for each of the networks the amount (volume) of coverage by party is equal for all statistical purposes, but that the valence (or

Table 5.4.   TV news biases by network

		d'	sd	n	t	p
CBS						
Overall		.034	.119	43	1.87	n.s.
	Volume	.010	.111	20	0.40	n.s.
	Valence	.055	.125	23	2.11	<.05
ABC						
Overall		.051	.149	35	2.02	n.s.
	Volume	.031	.141	16	0.88	n.s.
	Valence	.068	.157	19	1.89	n.s.
NBC						
Overall		.037	.151	35	1.45	n.s.
	Volume	−.014	.145	16	0.39	n.s.
	Valence	.080	.145	19	2.40	<.05
Fox News						
Overall		−.060	.115	9	1.57	n.s.
	Volume	−.082	.013	3	10.9	<.01
	Valence	−.026	.151	6	0.42	n.s.

tone) of coverage on the whole is pro-Democratic to a certain degree on both
NBC ($d' = .080$) and CBS ($d' = .055$).

Unlike the others, the aggregate of Fox News' coverage is negative, which
is to say, pro-Republican, in sign. The overall value ($d' = −.060$), it must
be noted, does not differ significantly from zero, and so is effectively equal
to zero. There is, however, a significant pro-Republican bias in the volume
of campaign coverage on Fox News ($d' = −.082$); the d' for valence is nonsignificant. Even if one takes the view that statistical testing is inappropriate
because it is all of Fox News' coverage that is being measured, not a sample
of it, the magnitude of d' for Fox News' coverage is just as small as it is in
many of the other tests we have conducted and reported previously. The overall d' of −.060 suggests that the coverage of the news content of Fox News is
53 percent Republican to 47 percent Democratic.

It should be noted, however, that while examinations of the broadcast networks date to 1968, Fox News' performance has only been measured for the
2004 and 2008 elections. To account for changes that might have taken place
across the decades, we also constructed a direct comparison of measurements
made by the same scholars inside the same studies (e.g. Zeldes et al., 2008;
Fico et al., 2008; CMPA, 2004; Lowry & Xie, 2007; Farnsworth & Lichter,
2009; PEJ, 2008; and CMPA, 2009). The performance of Fox News in covering the 2004 and 2008 presidential election campaigns was compared directly
to the performance of the network news broadcasts for those two campaigns,
yielding the result that Fox News' coverage was significantly more pro-
Republican than that of the broadcast networks ($t = 2.72, p < .05$).

The difference between Fox News and the broadcast networks is one of the largest differences we have uncovered in all of these studies, dwarfing virtually everything except the impact of an owner's politics on the outlet's content. (In fact, given the known political preferences of Rupert Murdoch, the chairman of the board of News Corp., the parent company of Fox News, this could be taken as more evidence of the same phenomenon.) However, the statement that "Fox News is more pro-Republican than the broadcast networks" is a relative statement, not an absolute one; in fact, the data presented by those recent scholars suggests that Fox News is closer to balanced ($d' = -.060$) than the networks ($d' = .089$). I am not prepared to make this conclusion. Unlike the other studies we have considered herein, this one summarizes studies conducted by a relatively small number of scholars using a limited number of methodologies across only two of the sixteen campaigns examined herein. It is clear that Fox News's reporting is to the right, politically speaking, of the networks, significantly and substantively so. Whether that is because Fox News is genuinely conservative or because the broadcast networks have drifted to the left, or some combination of the two is not yet clear, at least so far as empirical measurement is concerned.

Having explored some of the sources of, and specific questions regarding, media bias in coverage of presidential election campaigns, it is time to consider the implications of these findings. This is the task we will perform in chapter 6.

6

Conclusions, Caveats, and Ruminations

The debate about media bias revolves around two ad hoc models formulated by critics of the media and promulgated without either thorough reasoning or formal testing. The pervasiveness of each of them of them in the belief systems of Americans are reminiscent of Lippmann's (1922/1991) description of how false beliefs come into being: " . . . the casual fact, the creative imagination, the will to believe, and out of these three elements a counterfeit of reality . . . (p. 14)."

Conservatives argue that media are liberal because reporters in their capacities as private citizens express opinions supporting liberal positions and candidates. This is our casual fact. Once we have added to that fact the belief (true or not) that the media are inherently hostile to one's positions and the ability to point out specific elements of news media outside of the context of the complete coverage of a given issue (or in this case, campaign), and marry them to the logic of instance confirmation, the conclusion that the news media are liberal moves from mere conjecture to a strongly held personal belief.

This is not meant to denigrate people who hold to a conservative ideology, as liberals do exactly the same thing. They, too, have access to a casual fact: that owners/publishers as a class tend to be conservative in viewpoint. Once we have added to that fact the belief (true or not) that the media are inherently hostile to one's positions and the ability to point out specific elements of news media outside of the context of the complete coverage of a given issue (or in this case, campaign), and marry them to the logic of instance confirmation, the conclusion that the news media are conservative moves from mere conjecture to a strongly held personal belief.

101

Since sauce for the goose is sauce for the gander, it appears that for the most part both models are false. In the aggregate, "the media" as a body aren't biased against either end of the political spectrum.

Before continuing, it is critical to note that the conclusions that follow pertain solely to the domain we have been researching: the performance of the news media in covering presidential election campaigns. This particular issue is a special case in that, just as we were able to determine a metric for measuring this particular genre of news coverage, others have been able to as well, not simply researchers, but editors, ombudsmen, critics and the like. There is a lot of research on this topic—almost 100 studies subsumed in here—not solely because the outcomes of presidential campaigns are important (although they are) but also because coverage of presidential campaigns is relatively easy to measure. And if it is easy to measure, so, too, is it easy to monitor, which implies in turn that it is simpler for news media outlets to do a better job at arriving at balanced positions in covering presidential campaigns than they would in covering other, less cut-and-dried, issues. In short, this is a special case of a sort: it is distinctly possible that bias on other issues could be substantially larger than the amounts we have detected here.

That said, the data clearly indicates that the media, on the whole, with the exception of specific individual outlets on either side of the ideological spectrum (that have a strong tendency to offset one another), tend to be neither pro-Republican nor pro-Democrat in their coverage of Presidential election campaigns. On the whole the media are smack dab in the middle. This is the conclusion we reached in 2000 (D'Alessio & Allen, 2000), and that conclusion has not been affected by this expansion on that report.

How could this be, that after all the shouting is done, we can still say that coverage is unbiased on the whole? As we pointed out in chapter 2, any generalization about a social structure as complex as the news media industry that is based on a single fact concerning one element of that industry is likely to be untenable. The media have multiple identities, not just one. A news media outlet is not simply a big room with a pack of reporters running about willy-nilly saying whatever pleases their partisan souls, nor is it just a spider's web, an owner sitting in the middle pulling on strands in order to get his or her workers to perform on command. There are checks and balances on each of those actors that moderate their behaviors.

Several of these checks and balances work strongly toward positioning the news media in the middle of the road. One is manifestly economic: the ideological middle is where the most potential users are, and so the nature of a news media outlet as a business dictates that the outlet should stay near the middle of the road ideologically. Of course, it has been demonstrated theoretically that it is possible to make a profit with a news media outlet operating toward one end or the other of the ideological continuum (and in fact we have detected biased news media outlets that manage to stay in business). But what has to be recalled about this phenomenon is that a) it favors neither end of the political spectrum over the other, and so the biased outlet is as likely to be conservative as liberal and b) the successful operation of one outlet at one end of the ideological continuum opens up a viable market niche at the other end, as Sutter (2001) has pointed out. Once both niches are filled, the two outlets offset one another ideologically. Individual outlets, therefore, can be biased even as the aggregate is not. And this appears to be exactly what we have seen.

There are statistically significant variations in content, as we have also seen. Newspapers tend to give more coverage to Republican candidates, while both newspapers and TV network news tends to be more negative in tone toward them. These findings, too, are similar to those we found in 2000, and further, it remains true that although some of the measurements of bias are statistically significant, the deviations from balanced coverage are not particularly large in magnitude. A difference of a few percentage points either way from perfect balance in coverage is almost certainly undetectable to the average user, who, it must be recalled, does not process the entire body of coverage all at once at the end of a campaign as a researcher does. The user experiences it on a day-by-day basis across the entire period of the campaign, moderated by all the mechanical (go out and miss the news, dog eats the newspaper on Thursday) and cognitive (forgetting, selective exposure, selective categorization) processes that are involved with making sense of news reports. It seems likely that differences in content of the magnitude we discovered are indistinct to the user under those conditions.

At the same time, although it seems likely that the user does not notice biases of the magnitudes we have discovered, the truth is that no one knows. The question of the threshold level of bias an ordinary user can routinely detect has never been examined. The subjective nature of perceptions of bias in users suggests that a threshold would have to be relatively high in order to stand out from the perceptual noise created by processes such as selective categorization, but this conclusion is only an educated guess and nothing more. It certainly would be interesting to look into.

Oddly enough, it appears that at one time one of the competing visions of pervasive media bias—liberal or conservative—possessed more truth than the other. As we have seen, in campaigns before the 1976 election there was a strong association between a newspaper's editorial endorsement and the bias in its coverage. To a large degree papers endorsing Democrats had coverage favoring Democrats and papers endorsing Republicans had coverage endorsing Republicans. This would lend some credence to the conjecture by liberal critics of the news industries that claims that it is management that determines any biases seen in the content. (Indeed, one of the critics who commented on this, A. J. Liebling, was writing during this time period. As it happens, he was accurately reporting what he was seeing, as he so often did.) But times change and systems change; there are fewer and fewer newspapers every year, there is less competition in markets every year, and fewer and fewer papers make endorsements every year. Somewhere in this process, the association between endorsement and coverage appears to have disappeared.

This may be due to an unexpected consequence of the business nature of a newspaper: to the extent that a newspaper is operated as a business by people of business, management is disengaged from the day-to-day content of the paper. People of business, after all, are people of business, not journalists. Then, at endorsement time, the owners stop by to let the editors know who the paper will be backing in its editorial pages, and then they are off to the rest of their business holdings again, biases in coverage in the pages of the paper of no concern so long as the paper makes money.

In this report we have dealt with only two kinds of ownership, "private" ownership as a surrogate for a hands-on style of management (since the owner is presumed to desire to control the content of his or her news media outlet) and "public" ownership, which represents a hands-off owner presumed to be disengaged with day-to-day monitoring and having a preference for maximal profits as a return on investment. As we have seen just in passing, however, ownership is in truth a much too complex question to be explored in simple binary terms. There are news media outlets that are the property of enormous conglomerates (as ABC is the property of Disney) and who are their own corporations (as the Washington Post Company); there are certainly other corporate models in between. As we have seen, some, such as *The New York Times*, allow the public to foot the bill while the voting stock, board of directors and editorial control is vested in the same people who have always had it: the Ochs/Sulzberger families. There are co-op newspapers such as the *Milwaukee Journal-Sentinal* and newspapers owned and operated by non-profits, such as the *St. Petersburg Times*. There are privately owned newspapers started up specifically for political purposes (the *Washington Times*), privately owned papers that have been the property of one family for decades (the *Dallas Morning News*) and privately owned papers that are the property of someone who owns a dozen other businesses (as with Sam Zell's ownership of the Times-Mirror chain). A more in-depth study that finds a way to determine the locus of control over a paper's editorial policies might again find a relationship between editorial policies and coverage biases—one would expect that the closer an owner/publisher is to the day-to-day operations of the news media outlet in question, the more control the owner/publisher exerts—but the analysis herein suggests that the relationship between endorsement and coverage has disappeared by and large.

This points up another caveat we must present in considering our findings, that the number of studies of media coverage not only varies from campaign to campaign, but also that the number has been declining across the last several elections. Part of that is attributable to the mechanics of publication in the social sciences: a content analysis takes time to do properly. Then, once the research has been conducted and written up, it takes still more time for it to be run through the cycle of submission, review and revision that accompanies the publication process. It is almost a certainty that there are additional studies that would help elucidate the current relationship between ownership/endorsement and content being prepared, but we may not see them for years. It is a characteristic of the print media especially that they are not ephemeral; rather, they are printed and stored, and can be examined retrospectively, as did Batlin in examining the coverage of San Francisco's papers in 1892, and so studies of the media content of the 2008 election can be expected to be appearing in journals and on the Internet into the 2020s and beyond. But we do not have access to those future studies now.

As with the question of overall bias, when we considered the question of biases regarding incumbents, there were two predominant models or schools of thought. Scholars expecting a pro-incumbency bias pointed out the extra degree of access to the daily news hole that a sitting president possesses simply by dint of being president. At the same time scholars expecting an anti-incumbency bias pointed out that a sitting president is also to a degree a sitting duck who, as a requirement of being leader of the free world, must take actions that in turn open the president (as a candidate) to criticism.

Strangely enough, both of these models received a modicum of support. Incumbent presidents do get more coverage in newspapers than their challengers (reflecting the sitting president's greater access), but the coverage they receive in both newspapers and TV network news is more negative in tone, reflecting the criticism that takes place. (As an aside, it seems reasonable that incumbents get a greater proportion of space in newspapers than they do on TV news because television newscasters worked for years under the auspices of the Equal Time Provision, which basically required that they give the candidates equal time on the air; print media including newspapers had no such requirement.)

The caveat to the conclusion that both types of incumbency-related bias prediction models are supported is this: they appear to only be true if the incumbent is a Republican.

The findings on the valence of coverage of incumbents could be taken as the "smoking gun" that exposes the "liberal media conspiracy" once and for all (if one ignores their increased access to the news hole), but in truth that seems unlikely. First, it has to be recalled that there have been exactly six sitting Republican presidents who have stood for election during the course of this study: the elections of 1956 (Eisenhower) and 1976 (Ford) have been barely examined (return again to figure 1); coverage of the campaigns of 1972 (Nixon) and 1984 (Reagan) seem to have been relatively well balanced. The largest anti-incumbency effects have been seen in the campaigns of 1992 (Bush) and 2004 (Bush).

Interpreting this is problematic when we consider the number of things that the Presidents Bush have in common with each other and not with other Republicans in that group. Is there an anti-incumbent bias in these elections because they both are Republicans, indicating an actual pro-Democratic bias in the media? Or is it that they are both Yalies? From Texas? Oil men? Former aviators? None of these latter potential explanations seem particularly plausible, and I would not suggest that they are. My point is they represent uncontrolled variables in the analysis whose impact cannot be systematically eliminated; there are certainly other such variables, any one of which might explain the observed result.

Or is the explanation that the role of media in covering an election campaign has changed since the days of Dick Nixon, or even Ronnie Reagan? Certainly Farnsworth and Lichter (2007) have demonstrated increasing amounts of negativity in campaign coverage across time. Perhaps we have observed what appears to be an anti-Republican bias here simply because there were twice as many Republican incumbent presidents as Democratic ones in recent years. If all three of those recent incumbent campaigners—George H.W. Bush, Bill Clinton and George W. Bush—were covered with equal levels of negativity, the aggregate numbers would appear to have an anti-Republican bias. The answer to this will also have to wait: as it seems now, we will have a second Democratic incumbent running in 2012, and we cannot see the next Republican president standing for re-election any sooner than 2016.

A related concern is the data concerning Fox News. Prima facia, given the obvious and overwhelming editorial preferences of the channel, and that it has never been subject to either the Fairness Doctrine or the Equal Time Provision, it makes perfect sense that Fox News be situated to the right of other TV news sources. The data suggests that Fox News is indeed to the right politically of the broadcast networks, but that this is because Fox holds down the political center (or just barely to the right) while all three broadcast networks have drifted to the left. This seems unlikely. The logic of Sutter's (2001) argument applies as well here. For three networks to wage economic war over the left of the political spectrum, leaving the center and the entire right to one cable channel is an unviable economic strategy, doubly unlikely since the television networks are both the property of larger corporations, consequently making numerous content decisions (i.e., the producing and cancellation of entertainment shows) motivated by profits, and are also pressured annually by declining ratings (Straubhaar & Larose, 2006). Three network TV newscasts competing for the political left leaving the right completely open is a strategy of economic mutually assured suicide; it is hard to imagine their corporate parents sitting idly by while it happens.

This points up another concern of meta-analysis: it is dependent not only on the studies that are available but also on the methodologies of those studies. As noted in chapter 5, the Fox News analysis is based on a small number of studies conducted by a small number of researchers, whereas our other analyses are the product of larger numbers of different researchers and techniques. Whether Fox is truly the only channel still holding down the political center or not will be revealed when greater numbers of researchers using greater numbers of techniques have reported on their findings on a greater number of campaigns.

Similarly, when considering our findings herein about the nature of newspaper coverage, we have to recognize that that the majority of studies summarized here are studies of large, well-known outlets. Indeed, since a large proportion of the studies involve members of the Prestige Press, all of whom are both large (circulations in excess of 100,000) and well-known by definition, we were forced to consider them separately lest they systematically influence our conclusions.

There is evidence, herein and elsewhere, that the reliance of scholars on large newspapers may influence their, and subsequently our, conclusions. In table 5.1, for instance, we report 229 papers endorsing Republicans and 203 endorsing Democrats; historically endorsements have favored the Republican by a much greater degree (*Editor & Publisher*, 1996). The data supplied by Mitchell (2000) suggests a reason why: in 2000, 55 percent of large (circulation greater than 100,000) newspapers making endorsements endorsed George W. Bush. However, of small newspapers (circulation less than 50,000) who made endorsements (noting that 3 in 8 of them did not endorse), 72 percent endorsed Bush. Papers of intermediate size were in between, at 62 percent, suggesting that the differences are systematic.

The nature of the findings we present here are that they are robust against distinctions of this sort if the processes that underlie biases in coverage are the same in large and small newspapers. It seems reasonable that they are; the forces acting upon them are much the same. But that is only a presupposition. In the future it should be possible to test that presupposition empirically.

There are other questions that remain to be answered in the future. A critical one is the relationship between the politics of a given geographic area and coverage of elections in the local media. The very nature of concern about media bias is that, as Williams (1975) put it, media coverage is putatively influential; if it were not, no one would care. But at the same time, the economic nature of the media is such that the political center is a preferred location for media content. So: do the media influence political thinking in a given area, do they conform to the local politics of the region, are the two basically unrelated or are they interrelated, mutually influencing one another? Answering this relies on developing a means of estimating the political identity of a news media outlet's primary market. We are currently working on that and once a local area's political preferences can been established, we will be able to compare them to a given outlet's content, and determine the extent of interrelationship between the news media outlet and its locale.

Another area of media coverage of presidential campaigns that remains thoroughly unexamined is that of the foreign language and minority group media. Three of the studies of newspaper content each included one paper from the historically black media (Graber 1971 and 1976, used the *Chicago Daily Defender*; Millspaugh, 1949, the *Baltimore Afro-American*). No researcher to my knowledge has considered the political elements of news content in any of the Hispanic media, despite the fact that TV channels such as Univision and newspapers such as the New York-based *El Diario* reach hundreds of thousands of users weekly.

We also did not consider the associations, if any, between the textual elements of a news media report and the visual elements, choosing instead to simply combine them as being separate tests of the same report. In a way, it makes sense that they differ, in valence, perhaps if not in volume, in that they are created and prepared by different parts of a news media organization. Pictures and film/video are the product of the photographers and camerapersons who take them, not of the reporter reading and/or writing the text. The use of visual elements is as often a product of the art department as the news department. Being products of different operational sections of the same outlet, the potential exists for the text and the visuals to be sending different messages depending on the preferences, biases and background of the different staffs of those sections.

In short, we have covered a great deal of ground in the analyses conducted for this report, but a great deal of ground remains unexplored.

KICKING DICK NIXON?

That said, we can now return to Richard Nixon, in the Cadoro Room of the Beverly Hilton the day after he loses the 1962 election for governor of California, telling the gathered reporters that they won't have Dick Nixon to kick around any more. The question asks itself: Did the press actually kick Dick Nixon around?

Oddly, so far as this study is concerned the answer to that is unknown. The simplistic response is that the gubernatorial election in California is not a presidential election in the United States, and that this book is concerned with presidential elections. That is a cheap and easy answer, however, and it presupposes that information gained about presidential elections is not applicable to elections at other levels.

A second answer is that we cannot tell, not because the election is at the gubernatorial level, but because, to the best of my knowledge, no one has ever formally looked at coverage of the 1962 campaign for governor of California. (Ambrose, 1987, described it as "fair," but presents no data in support of this conclusion.) As we have pointed out before, it is a critical disadvantage of meta-analysis that it depends on the existence of previous studies of an issue. If no one has studied the 1962 campaign coverage in California previously, then we cannot aggregate their (nonexistent) results in order to draw conclusions specifically about the campaign's coverage. Of course, such studies could be conducted: many of the newspapers covering the campaign have had their content archived in microfilm, and while TV newscasts of the campaign have largely disappeared, TV news was in its infancy and probably not crucial to the campaign. But until someone conducts these studies, meta-analysis of their results cannot be conducted.

We can apply what we have learned generally to this specific situation, of course. We know that under the conditions that applied in 1962, before the reforms engendered by the Watergate era and before the major tendency for news media outlets, particularly newspapers, to be publicly owned and to not make endorsements of candidates, that there is a good chance that coverage actually favored Nixon. When he ran for president in 1960, 68 percent of California newspapers endorsed him, as opposed to 21 percent endorsing John Kennedy and 11 percent not endorsing (Brown, 1960), and in those days, as we have seen in chapter 5, the endorsement made by a given paper and the bias of its coverage were related about three-quarters of the time. While we know that the *Los Angeles Times* had gone to extraordinary lengths to ensure that its coverage would be completely neutral, these measures are noteworthy in part because they were unusual at the time, and it seems likely that most news media outlets did not make such efforts; in fact, most outlets still do not make such efforts. On the whole, it seems reasonable to presume that media coverage actually favored Nixon in his campaign for governor of California, but that is only a presumption, not a demonstrable fact.

We can also look at the coverage he received as a Presidential candidate. The aggregate d' for Nixon's coverage for his three Presidential campaigns was close to neutral but actually favorable to him ($d' = -.041$, $p < .05$; recall that a negative d' in this context indicates favoritism to the Republican) to the extent that it is unbalanced. Of course, this includes the coverage of the 1968 and 1972 campaigns, (which were yet to come from the perspective of 1962) but even the 1960 coverage was somewhat favorable to him (three of the four measures were positive, that is, pro-Kennedy, but they are swamped in magnitude by Danielson and Adams' (1961) examination of selection bias in 69 newspapers).

So why was Nixon so bitter on that day in 1962? Nixon, of course, was in some ways a special case. He had not only lost the 1962 campaign but also the 1960 presidential race as well. Worse for him, the opponents he was looking forward to running against for the 1964 Republican nomination—Rockefeller and Romney—had outdone him. The bitterness of his disappointment must have been almost unprecedented.

But why should he blame the media for this loss? For what reason are political candidates, and particularly losing political candidates ranging chronologically from Adlai Stevenson to John McCain, so vociferous in their claims of media bias? Recall from chapter 4 that newspapers provide slightly more coverage to Republican candidates and the tone of television network news is slight preferential to Democrats. On the whole, these offset one another and the overall tenor of media coverage is virtually as balanced as it can be within our capability to measure it. The only truly systematic partisan bias detected, in chapter 5, was that television news tends to be rougher on Republican incumbents than Democratic—but of the six Republican incumbents across the period of this study, only George H.W. Bush lost a reelection campaign that he should have had reasonable expectation of being able to win. (Ford, of course, also failed of election, but it is worth noting that he had not been elected in the first place, and the position of the Republican Party in the years immediately following the Watergate scandal was largely untenable.) So why the constant, and largely incorrect, complaints?

Accusations of Bias

As we have discussed, while the media are not simplistic organizations whose behavior can be accurately predicted by focusing on one small element of their makeup, so too are politicians complex beings who bring a multitude of perceptions and motivations to their pronouncements regarding the behavior of the news media. We can summarize some of the important perceptions and motivations by recalling two major aspects of a Presidential candidate:

that the candidate is the figurehead of a campaign, and that the candidate is a person. We will treat these in the reverse order.

That a candidate is a person seems self-evident, but at the same time it does not seem to have been taken into account very often. Presidential candidates are rarely, if ever, participants in experiments conducted by scholars in the fields of communication, political science or psychology, at least not once they have achieved national prominence. We are left to speculate hypothetically about their reasoning processes or attempt to discern them from the pages of their memoirs, but as people they are almost certainly as subject to the hostile media effect as any college sophomore participating in an experiment. Further, as Gunther and Schmitt (2004) point out, studies of the hostile media effect are routinely done with participants who are engaged with the topic. This is specifically because engaged persons are expected to be responsive to media content in a way that the disengaged are not. In terms of ego-involvement and personal effort, there are very few people more engaged with a political campaign's news coverage than the candidates themselves generally are, and so it is not unreasonable to conclude that candidates are even more subject to the hostile media effect than people that are merely interested in and feel strongly about an issue.

Further, as people of sufficient prominence that their public statements are considered newsworthy, the complaints of presidential candidates are heard and taken seriously in a way that those of most private citizens are not. For instance, Jamieson (2000) has compiled many of Bob Dole's comments on *The New York Times*, and they are indeed bitter, but there is nothing there that many of us have not also said in the privacy of our homes when we are presented with news content with which we vociferously disagree. The only difference is that there were newspaper and television reporters present to record Senator Dole's words and not yours or mine.

When considering the nature of a candidate as a person, it is also important to recognize that a person who desires the office of president of the United States, the putative leader of the free world, has to possess another critical characteristic, and that is faith in one's own vision. As we pointed out in chapter 4, each candidate has spent years in public service and every one of them has already risen to a position of power and authority. Campaigning for the presidency is a cruel and grueling process that literally occupies years of one's life. To make that sort of personal sacrifice, candidates must of necessity firmly believe that their policies are better for the nation than those of their opponent; they must believe that they are right and their opponents are wrong.

Unfortunately, both major party presidential candidates are convinced they are right and one of them is going to lose. This is a situation that the loser must reconcile to, cognitively and emotionally. Mentally, the process almost certainly includes the following stage: I, the candidate, was presenting the best vision of the future for my country, so how is it that the voters have rejected it and me?

Again, there have been no psychological surveys of losing presidential candidates, but historically there are parallels: in the book of Leviticus, Moses is told to tell his brother Aaron to " . . . lay both his hands upon the head of the live goat and confess over him all the iniquities of the children of Israel, and all their transgressions in all their sins, putting them on the head of the goat, and shall send him away by the hand of a fit man into the wilderness" (Leviticus, 16:21).

This goat is, of course, the scapegoat. The sins of the people are placed upon him and he is driven into the wilderness to take the sins away. The goat did not commit the sins, but he carries the blame for all. Thus the term "scapegoat" came to us, to indicate the one who is taking the blame for failure, deserved or not.

That political scapegoating occurs is fairly obvious. The mutual recriminations between the McCain and Palin camps following the 2008 campaign were particularly public and unattractive (c.f. Bumiller, 2008), and point up the fact that the press is not the only entity available to cast blame upon. But the news media are ubiquitously there, too, readily available to be accused of having had an unfair bias against the losing campaign. It is a natural, human response to the rejection of one's self and one's policies to blame someone for that rejection, and, as Halberstam (1979) has pointed out, if the finger of blame cannot be pointed at Nixon (or any other candidate), then at whom?

Returning to our second main point here, it must be recalled that, apart from whatever personal feelings the candidate has about media coverage, the candidate is also the figurehead and most prominent spokesperson of a campaign organization consisting of thousands of people. This gives the candidate two more reasons to consider "giving the business" to the media regardless of the media's actual performance. Campaigns, of course, are staffed by people; some of them are professionals, but a large number are volunteers as well. If the campaign workers tire of their jobs or slip in their enthusiasm, the campaign runs the risk of losing the election on simply mechanical grounds: by not getting their voters to the booths on Election Day. One way to motivate the workers is to create the "us versus the world" mentality. That is, to create a sense of teamwork on the part of the workers by framing the campaign, candidate and workers as an underdog community needing to work in unison in order to overcome all the forces acting against it, one of which forces can be identified, fairly or unfairly, as the media. In fact, as we have seen, this strategy dates back at least to the Truman administration (Ross, 1968).

Similarly, to the extent that voters identify with the campaign, they can share in the feeling of being "part of the team," which should in turn increase their participation in terms of both donation and voting. In fact, mobilization, of volunteers and voters, is one of the goals of the campaign's communications (Foot & Schneider, 2002; Heinlein, 1992), and the underdog is generally an attractive person for people to rally around simply by dint of being the underdog. It should be obvious that one way to achieve underdog status is to claim that "the media are out to get us," whether or not they actually are. After all, it is the perception that counts, as perceptions of media bias are often unrelated to the reality of coverage (see chapter 2).

It is speculation, of course, but there is possibly one more strategic reason for a candidate to make charges of media bias during the course of a campaign, and that would be in the hope of getting reporters to modify their behavior to the candidate's benefit. The notion of "working the umpires" or "working the referees" is engrained in professional sports, which are another example of a classic "win-lose"-type game that a political campaign is. Weaver (1984) makes the point that arguing with umpires is intended to cause them to work harder and reflect more thoroughly on their performance. In the case of a reporter, the same impact could potentially cause them to moderate their use of language regarding a given campaign.

Interestingly enough, ex post facto, Nixon said almost exactly that in his memoirs (Nixon, 1978) in reference to his 1962 tongue-lashing of the press: "I believe that it gave the media a warning that I would not sit back and take whatever was dished out to me. In that respect, I think that the episode was partly responsible for the much fairer treatment I received from the press during the next few years . . . " (p. 246). As noted above, his coverage was slightly favorable toward him in his subsequent campaigns.

It might be possible to examine this by focusing on four of the campaigns that were most vociferous about attempting to register protest about their coverage: the campaigns of Stevenson in 1952 ("One Party Press"); Nixon in 1972 ("Nattering Nabobs of Negativism"); Bush in 1992 ("Annoy the Media") and Dole in 1996 ("Arm of the DNC"). (It could have been useful to have included Truman's campaign in 1948, but it has been much more poorly researched than the listed campaigns.) We recoded the measured d's such that a positive score indicated a bias in favor of the campaign lodging the complaints, and examined the volume and valence of the newspaper and television coverage each of the protesting campaigns received.

As it happens, those campaigns did not get good coverage, at least on television network news. The protesting campaigns were discussed in more negative terms than their opponents (for valence of television network news coverage, $d' = -.084$; $p < .05$; there were no significant differences from balanced coverage for newspaper coverage or the volume of television coverage).

This may mean that the candidates in question had good cause to complain, but having cause to complain is not necessarily a valid strategic reason to risk the possible consequences of calling out the news media. That is, what we can't tell is whether the tone of coverage was better before the complaints, better after, or remained the same. It is possible that the candidates had good reason to complain. Or it might be that, in complaining about nothing, they turned the TV networks against them. Or some combination of the two.

The strategic point of "working the refs" is to moderate the treatment that you receive from them. The data sets we have access to are not dense enough in time for us to determine whether or not coverage biases were present before the candidates' attacks or whether they moderated after. The point is, however, that complaining about the media is a strategic option available to candidates in their attempts to manage their images and coverage, and some candidates (or some campaigns) chose that option.

FUTURE OF CHARGES OF BIAS

It seems likely that, regardless of the data presented, people will continue to complain that the media are biased politically against the presidential candidate of their choice. First of all, the psychological processes that underlie the charges are transparent to the people involved. There is a reason that instance confirmation is a fairly common phenomenon, and that is that it is a simple and apparently logical way to reason. "Prove it!" demands one person, and "Okay, here's proof," replies the other, pointing at a single instance of media content that he or she believes substantiates his or her claim. (At that, given selective perception, or selective categorization, as one prefers, these two people may not even agree on the meaning of that single item.) It requires statistical reasoning and the ability to look at political coverage as a complete corpus rather than one report at a time before judgments of bias ought to be made. But these are tools that most people do not use, and rightfully so. Should people be expected to keep every newspaper they read, to record every newscast they watch, in order to express an opinion on a topic?

Similarly, as we have seen, the charge of bias is a very convenient tune in the political repertoire. Whether the politician in question legitimately believes it to be true or not—and there is no evidence to suggest that politicians do not believe the media are biased and good reason (the known consequences of the hostile media effect) to believe that they do believe it—a charge of bias serves, as we have seen, as a call to arms for campaign workers and supporters alike and challenges the media themselves to examine their own conduct more carefully. The media also provide a convenient scapegoat for failure, ubiquitously available to be driven into the wilderness when the candidate cannot blame him or herself.

So ultimately, given that it is unlikely that any discernable differences in the conduct of, or beliefs about, presidential campaign coverage will result from this research, what is the point? Is there a purpose to kicking Dick Nixon one more time, years after he has gone to his reward?

The answer to that is twofold. First, by examining the presence and magnitude of media bias, we can start to understand the processes by which systematic regularities in media content start to come about, which elements of their multitudinous natures force their news content to the ideological right, which to the left, and which firmly to the center. If any. This study is only one small step in that direction. There is yet a great deal more work to do.

And second, the fact that people now take for granted the reasoning processes that lead them to the conclusion that the media are not only biased but indeed biased against them, does not mean that these reasoning processes must of necessity continue to be used. It is as important to know how people reason incorrectly as it is to know how they reason correctly. Once we understand that, it is possible that we can learn to teach people to reason correctly and accurately.

To do this requires accurate knowledge. It is no use to make guesses about media content. It is necessary to measure what is out there (and how it is changing over time), so that, when we add our creative imagination and will to believe to our available facts on a subject, we arrive at a correct, rather than counterfeit, version of reality.

As we have seen, it is critical to the democratic process that the news media provide unbiased coverage of election campaigns and candidates. It is necessary to the functioning of a representative democracy. Without it, the electorate will neither be able to arrive at rational voting decisions nor evaluate seated representatives and enacted policies. In the case of the election campaigns, at least, for the most part they do.

Appendix A

THE MASTER ANALYSIS TABLE

The overall analysis was conducted on the following set of data. "Study" is a reference to one of the studies referenced below the table. For "Medium," NP is newspapers, TV is television and NM is newsmagazines. The "Type of Bias" is a measure of volumetric, valence or selection bias as discussed in chapter 3; "Num" or "Number" refers to a count of stories while "Amt" means an amount of space, measured in column inches or seconds of air time or the like. "N" is the number of news media outlets examined in that particular study. "d'" is the d' statistic as calculated per chapter 3 and "Year" refers to the particular presidential campaign being examined. Note that some studies can examine multiple media or multiple campaigns and are therefore reported multiple times in the table.

Table A.1. Master Analysis Table

Study	Medium	Type of Bias	N	d'	Year
Millspaugh (1949)	NP	Volume/Amt	4	-0.302	1948
Berelson et al. (1954)	NP	Valence/Num	3	-0.167	1948
Klein & Maccoby (1954)	NP	Volume/Photo	8	−0.181	1952
Klein & Maccoby (1954)	NP	Volume/Num	8	−0.084	1952
Klein & Maccoby (1954)	NP	Volume/Amt	8	−0.071	1952
Klein & Maccoby (1954)	NP	Valence/Num	8	0.070	1952
Batlin (1954)	NP	Valence/Amt	3	−0.217	1952
Batlin (1954)	NP	Volume/Photo	3	−0.356	1952
Higbie (1954)	NP	Volume/Photo	13	−0.305	1952
Higbie (1954)	NP	Volume/Num	14	−0.104	1952
Blumberg (1954)	NP	Volume/Photo	35	−0.066	1952
Blumberg (1954)	NP	Volume/Num	35	0.048	1952
Blumberg (1954)	NP	Volume/Amt	35	0.018	1952
Kobre (1953)	NP	Volume/Photo	34	0.069	1952
Kobre (1953)	NP	Volume/Num	34	0.023	1952
Kobre (1953)	NP	Volume/Amt	34	0.017	1952
Nollet (1968)	NP	Volume/Amt	1	0.053	1952
Price (1954)	NP	Volume/Amt	8	−0.072	1952
Price (1954)	NP	Selection	8	−0.015	1952
Vavreck (2003)	NP	Volume/Num	1	−0.042	1952
Repass & Chaffee (1968)	NP	Volume/Amt	8	−0.082	1956
Nollet (1968)	NP	Volume/Amt	1	0.094	1956
Vavreck (2003)	NP	Volume/Num	1	0.311	1956
Stempel (1961)	NP	Volume/Num	15	0.018	1960
Stempel (1961)	NP	Volume/Amt	15	0.003	1960
Nollet (1968)	NP	Volume/Amt	1	0.183	1960
Vavreck (2003)	NP	Volume/Num	1	0.034	1960
Danielson & Adams (1961)	NP	Selection	69	−0.052	1960
Repass & Chaffee (1968)	NP	Volume/Amt	8	−0.068	1964
Stempel (1965)	NP	Volume/Num	15	0.036	1964
Stempel (1965)	NP	Volume/Amt	15	0.035	1964
Nollet (1968)	NP	Volume/Amt	1	0.009	1964
Vavreck (2003)	NP	Volume/Num	1	−0.176	1964
Stempel (1969)	NP	Volume/Num	15	0.043	1968
Stempel (1969)	NP	Volume/Amt	15	0.049	1968

Study	Medium	Type of Bias	N	d'	Year
Graber (1971)	NP	Volume/Num	20	−0.229	1968
Vavreck (2003)	NP	Volume/Num	1	0.056	1968
Adatto (1990)	TV	Volume/Num	3	0.121	1968
Adatto (1990)	TV	Volume/Amt	3	0.183	1968
Stevenson et al. (1973)	TV	Volume/Amt	1	0.135	1968
Stevenson et al. (1973)	TV	Valence/Num	1	0.026	1968
Evarts & Stempel (1974)	NM	Valence	3	−0.109	1972
Evarts & Stempel (1974)	NP	Valence/Amt	6	0.124	1972
Graber (1976)	NP	Volume/Num	20	−0.328	1972
Hofstetter (1978)	NP	Volume/Num	2	−0.197	1972
Hofstetter (1978)	NP	Volume/Amt	2	−0.192	1972
Hofstetter (1978)	NP	Valence/Num	2	−0.038	1972
Hofstetter (1978)	NP	Valence/Amt	2	−0.027	1972
Meadow (1973)	NP	Volume/Num	3	0.226	1972
Vavreck (2003)	NP	Volume/Num	1	0.276	1972
Doll & Bradley (1974)	TV	Volume/Num	3	0.043	1972
Doll & Bradley (1974)	TV	Volume/Amt	3	0.000	1972
Evarts & Stempel (1974)	TV	Valence	3	0.097	1972
Malaney & Buss (1979)	TV	Volume/Num	1	0.058	1972
Malaney & Buss (1979)	TV	Volume/Amt	1	0.098	1972
Malaney & Buss (1979)	TV	Valence/Num	1	0.048	1972
Malaney & Buss (1979)	TV	Valence/Amt	1	−0.038	1972
Lowry (1974)	TV	Volume/Num	3	−0.190	1972
Lowry (1974)	TV	Volume/Amt	3	−0.017	1972
Frank (1973)	TV	Volume/Amt	3	0.341	1972
Hofstetter & Zukin (1979)	TV	Volume/Num	3	0.072	1972
Hofstetter & Zukin (1979)	TV	Valence	3	−0.043	1972
Hofstetter (1978)	TV	Volume/Num	3	0.074	1972
Hofstetter (1978)	TV	Volume/Amt	3	0.286	1972
Hofstetter (1978)	TV	Valence/Num	3	−0.181	1972
Hofstetter (1978)	TV	Valence/Amt	3	−0.030	1972
Meadow (1973)	TV	Volume/Amt	3	0.226	1972
Woodard (1994)	TV	Volume/Num	3	−0.046	1972
Einsiedel & Bibbee (1979)	NM	Volume	3	0.026	1976
Alverez & Glasgow (1997)	NP	Volume/Number	1	−0.105	1976
Vavreck (2003)	NP	Volume/Num	1	0.130	1976
Woodard (1994)	TV	Volume/Number	3	−0.233	1976
Friedman et al. (1980)	TV	Valence	3	0.006	1976

Study	Medium	Type of Bias	N	d'	Year
Alverez (1997)	NP	Volume/Num	1	0.068	1980
Alverez & Glasgow (1997)	NP	Volume/Num	1	−0.041	1980
Stempel & Windhauser (1984)	NP	Volume/Num	14	0.001	1980
Stempel & Windhauser (1984)	NP	Volume/Amt	14	−0.027	1980
Stovall (1985)	NP	Volume/Photo	50	−0.077	1980
Stovall (1985)	NP	Volume/Num	50	−0.042	1980
Stovall (1985)	NP	Volume/Amt	50	−0.022	1980
Vavreck (2003)	NP	Volume/Num	1	−0.051	1980
Stovall (1985)	NP	Selection	50	0.054	1980
Robinson (1983)	TV	Volume/Amt	1	−0.012	1980
Robinson (1983)	TV	Valence/Num	1	−0.050	1980
Robinson & Sheehan (1983)	TV	Valence	1	−0.106	1980
Woodard (1994)	TV	Volume/Num	3	−0.182	1980
Moriarty & Garramone (1987)	NM	Volume	3	−0.025	1984
Moriarty & Garramone (1987)	NM	Valence	3	−0.014	1984
Stempel (1991)	NM	Volume/Num	3	−0.172	1984
Stempel (1991)	NM	Valence/Num	3	−0.224	1984
Semetko, et al. (1991)	NP	Volume/Num	2	−0.079	1984
Stovall (1988)	NP	Volume/Photo	49	−0.094	1984
Stovall (1988)	NP	Volume/Num	49	−0.078	1984
Stovall (1988)	NP	Selection	49	−0.078	1984
Stempel & Windhauser (1991)	NP	Volume/Num	17	−0.126	1984
Stempel & Windhauser (1991)	NP	Valence/Num	17	0.074	1984
Vavreck (2003)	NP	Volume/Num	1	0.036	1984
Clancey & Robinson (1985)	TV	Valence	3	0.662	1984
Mullin, et al. (1986)	TV	Valence	3	−0.057	1984
Robinson (1985)	TV	Volume/Amt	3	0.027	1984
Semetko, et al. (1991)	TV	Volume/Num	3	0.011	1984
Windhauser & Evarts (1991)	TV	Volume/Num	3	−0.078	1984
Windhauser & Evarts (1991)	TV	Valence	3	−0.001	1984
Woodard (1994)	TV	Volume/Num	3	0.013	1984
Moriarty & Popovich (1991)	NM	Volume/Num	3	−0.155	1988
Moriarty & Popovich (1991)	NM	Valence	3	−0.162	1988
Patterson (1989)	NM	Valence	2	−0.250	1988
Popovich et al. (1993)	NM	Volume	3	0.127	1988
Popovich et al. (1993)	NM	Valence	3	−0.154	1988

Study	Medium	Type of Bias	N	d'	Year
Stempel (1991)	NM	Volume/Num	3	−0.039	1988
Stempel (1991)	NM	Valence/Num	3	−0.057	1988
Kenney & Simpson (1993)	NP	Volume/Photo	2	−0.318	1988
Kenney & Simpson (1993)	NP	Volume/Num	2	−0.328	1988
Kenney & Simpson (1993)	NP	Selection	2	−0.231	1988
Kenney & Simpson (1993)	NP	Valence/Num	2	−0.036	1988
Stempel & Windhauser (1989)	NP	Volume/Amt	14	−0.020	1988
Stempel & Windhauser (1991)	NP	Volume/Num	17	−0.079	1988
Stempel & Windhauser (1991)	NP	Valence/Num	17	−0.011	1988
Vavreck (2003)	NP	Volume/Num	1	0.154	1988
Adatto (1990)	TV	Volume/Num	3	0.038	1988
Adatto (1990)	TV	Volume/Amt	3	0.008	1988
Buchanan (1991)	TV	Volume/Num	5	−0.047	1988
Buchanan (1991)	TV	Valence	5	−0.385	1988
CMPA (1988)	TV	Volume/Num	3	0.017	1988
CMPA (1988)	TV	Valence	3	−0.037	1988
Windhauser & Everts (1991)	TV	Volume/Num	3	−0.082	1988
Windhauser & Everts (1991)	TV	Valence	3	0.056	1988
Woodard (1994)	TV	Volume/Num	3	−0.078	1988
McCord & Weaver (1996)	NM	Volume	3	0.017	1992
McCord & Weaver (1996)	NM	Valence	3	0.234	1992
Cavanaugh (1995)	NP	Volume/Amt	1	−0.234	1992
Cavanaugh (1995)	NP	Valence/Num	1	0.218	1992
Dalton et al. (1998)	NP	Volume/Num	46	−0.138	1992
Dalton et al. (1998)	NP	Volume/Photos	46	−0.061	1992
Dalton et al. (1998)	NP	Valence/Num	46	0.124	1992
Fan (1996)	NP	Volume/Amt	16	−0.034	1992
Fan (1996)	NP	Valence/Amt	16	0.048	1992
Hayes (2008)	NP	Valence	43	0.038	1992
Hayes (2010)	NP	Selection	43	−0.068	1992
King (1995)	NP	Valence/Num	3	−0.024	1992
Mantler & Whiteman (1995)	NP	Volume/Amt	6	−0.064	1992
Shaw & Sparrow (1999)	NP	Valence	41	0.049	1992
Staten & Sloss (1993)	NP	Volume/Num	1	−0.019	1992
Staten & Sloss (1993)	NP	Valence/Num	1	0.040	1992
Vavreck (2003)	NP	Volume/Num	1	−0.034	1992
Cavanaugh (1995)	TV	Volume/Amt	3	−0.146	1992

Study	Medium	Type of Bias	N	d'	Year
Cavanaugh (1995)	TV	Valence	3	0.093	1992
CMPA (1992)	TV	Volume/Num	3	−0.154	1992
CMPA (1992)	TV	Valence	3	0.109	1992
Hayes (2010)	TV	Selection	3	−0.048	1992
Joslyn & Ceccoli (1996)	TV	Volume/Num	3	−0.045	1992
Joslyn & Ceccoli (1996)	TV	Valence	3	0.540	1992
Lowry & Shidler (1995)	TV	Volume/Amt	4	0.037	1992
Lowry & Shidler (1995)	TV	Valence	4	0.091	1992
Lowry & Shidler (1998)	TV	Valence/Amt	4	0.086	1992
Shaw (1999)	TV	Valence	3	0.043	1992
Domke et al. (1997)	NP	Volume/Num	41	0.118	1996
Domke et al. (1997)	NP	Valence/Num	41	0.012	1996
Fico & Cote (1999)	NP	Valence	9	−0.250	1996
Hayes (2008)	NP	Valence	8	0.017	1996
Hayes (2010)	NP	Selection	6	−0.019	1996
Jamieson (2000)	NP	Volume/Photos	1	−0.135	1996
Jamieson (2000)	NP	Volume/Num	1	−0.080	1996
Lee et al. (2004)	NP	Volume/Photos	1	−0.123	1996
Vavreck (2003)	NP	Volume/Num	1	−0.103	1996
Waldman & DeVitt (1998)	NP	Volume/Photos	5	−0.034	1996
Waldman & DeVitt (1998)	NP	Valence/Photos	5	0.068	1996
CMPA (1996)	TV	Volume/Num	3	0.129	1996
CMPA (1996)	TV	Valence	3	0.148	1996
Hayes (2010)	TV	Selection	3	0.007	1996
Just (1997)	TV	Volume/Amt	3	0.156	1996
Just (1997)	TV	Valence	3	−0.144	1996
Lowry & Shidler (1998)	TV	Valence/Amt	4	0.087	1996
Murphy (1998)	TV	Volume/Num	3	0.016	1996
Murphy (1998)	TV	Valence	3	0.080	1996
Shaw (1999)	TV	Valence	3	0.021	1996
Hooker et al. (2001)	NM	Volume/Num	3	0.122	2000
Fisher (2001)	NP	Valence/Num	1	0.077	2000
Hayes (2008)	NP	Valence	12	−0.009	2000
Lee (2002)	NP	Volume/Num	2	−0.144	2000
P.E.J. (2000)	NP	Volume/Num	4	0.060	2000
Pritchard (2002)	NP	Valence	10	0.027	2000

Study	Medium	Type of Bias	N	d'	Year
Vavreck (2003)	NP	Volume/Num	1	−0.053	2000
Wang (2003)	NP	Valence/Num	2	−0.273	2000
Banning & Coleman (2009)	TV	Volume/Photos	3	−0.023	2000
Banning & Coleman (2009)	TV	Valence	3	0.106	2000
CMPA (2000)	TV	Valence	3	0.030	2000
Lichter (2001)	TV	Valence	1	0.010	2000
P.E.J. (2000)	TV	Volume/Num	5	0.070	2000
Zaldes, et al. (2008)	TV	Valence	3	−0.013	2000
Miller (2005)	NM	Volume/Num	3	−0.212	2004
Cummings (2006)	NP	Valence/Num	2	0.010	2004
McCluskey (2005)	NP	Volume/Num	2	0.046	2004
McCluskey (2005)	NP	Valence/Num	2	0.102	2004
Terry (2005)	Radio	Valence/Amt	3	−0.073	2004
Terry (2005)	Radio	Valence/Num	3	−0.085	2004
CMPA (2004)	TV	Valence	4	0.098	2004
Fico et al. (2008)	TV	Valence	6	0.055	2004
Zeldes et al. (2008)	TV	Valence	3	0.009	2004
Kim (2009)	NP	Volume/Num	2	0.223	2008
Kim (2009)	NP	Valence/Num	2	0.032	2008
Lee (2010)	NP	Volume/Num	2	−0.006	2008
Lee (2010)	NP	Valence/Num	2	0.150	2008
Lee (2010)	NP	Volume/Photos	2	−0.011	2008
PEJ (2008)	NP	Volume/Num	13	−0.060	2008
PEJ (2008)	NP	Valence/Num	13	0.328	2008
Beucker et al. (2009)	TV	Volume/Num	3	−0.043	2008
Beucker et al. (2009)	TV	Volume/Amt	3	−0.090	2008
CMPA (2009)	TV	Valence	4	0.265	2008
Farnsworth & Lichter (2011)	TV	Volume/Num	4	−0.120	2008
PEJ (2008)	TV	Volume/Num	6	−0.120	2008
PEJ (2008)	TV	Valence/Num	6	0.197	2008
Benoit et al. (2005)	NP	Valence/Num	13	0.090	Several
Lowry & Xie (2007)	TV	Valence	13	0.010	Several

124 *Appendix A*

STUDIES INCLUDED IN THE ANALYSIS

Adatto, K. (1990). Sound Bite Democracy: Network Evening News Presidential Campaign Coverage, 1968 and 1988. Research Paper R-2, Joan Shorenstein Barone Center for Press, Politics and Public Policy.
Alverez, R. M. (1997). *Information and Elections.* Ann Arbor, MI: University of Michigan Press.
Alverez, R. M., & Glasgow, G. (1997). Do Voters Learn from Presidential Election Campaigns? California Institute of Technology Division of Humanities and Social Sciences Working Paper #1022. [Online.] Downloaded 9/16/10 from http://www.hss.caltech.edu/SSPapers/wp1022.pdf.
Banning, S. A., & Coleman, R. (2009). A content analysis of presidential candidates' televised nonverbal communication. *Visual Communication Quarterly,* 16, 4–17.
Batlin, R. (1954). San Francisco newspapers' campaign coverage: 1896, 1952. *Journalism Quarterly,* 31, 297–303.
Benoit, W. L., Stein, K. A., & Hansen, G. J. (2005). *New York Times* coverage of presidential campaigns. *Journalism and Mass Communication Quarterly,* 82, 356–376.
Berelson, B. R., Lazarsfeld, P. F., & McPhee, W. N. (1954). *Voting: A Study of Opinion Formation in a Presidential Campaign.* Chicago: University of Chicago Press.
Beucker, M., Lambert, D., Makely, C., McKeague, M., Morgan, K., & Leidman, M.B. (2009). Lingering questions: The Fairness Doctrine and the 2008 presidential campaign coverage in western Pennsylvania. Paper presented to the Laurel Highlands Communication Conference.
Blumberg, N. B. (1954). *One Party Press? Coverage of the 1952 Presidential Campaign in 35 Daily Newspapers.* Lincoln, NB: University of Nebraska Press.
Buchanan, B. (1991). *Electing a President: The Markle Commission Research on Campaign 88.* Austin, TX: University of Texas Press.
Cavanaugh, J. W. (1995). *Media Effects of Voters: A Panel Study of the 1992 Presidential Election.* Lanham, MD: University Press of America.
Center for Media and Public Affairs (1988). Bad news is good news for Bush: TV coverage of the 1988 general election. *Media Monitor,* II(9).
Center for Media and Public Affairs (1992). Clinton's the one: TV news coverage of the 1992 general election. *Media Monitor,* VI(9).
Center for Media and Public Affairs (1996). Campaign 1996 final: How TV news covered the general election. *Media Monitor,* X(6).
Center for Media and Public Affairs (2000). Campaign 2000 final: How TV news covered the general election campaign. *Media Monitor,* XIV(6).
Center for Media and Public Affairs (2004). Campaign 2004 final: How TV news covered the general election campaign. *Media Monitor,* XVIII(6).
Center for Media and Public Affairs (2009). Election watch: Campaign 2008 final: How TV news covered the general election campaign. *Media Monitor,* XXIII(1).
Clancey, M., & Robinson, M. J. (1985). The media in campaign 1984: General election coverage Part I. *Public Opinion,* 8, 49–54, 59.

Cummings, J. E. (2006). Unbalanced media coverage and the 2004 presidential election: *The New York Times* vs. the *Washington Times*. Unpublished master's thesis, University of Alabama.

Dalton, R. J., Beck, P. A., & Huckfeldt, R. (1998). Partisan cues and the media: Information flows in the 1992 Presidential election. *The American Political Science Review*, 92, 111–126.

Danielson, W. A., & Adams, J. B. (1961). Completeness of press coverage of the 1960 campaign. *Journalism Quarterly*, 38, 441–452.

Doll, H. D., & Bradley, B. E. (1974). A study of the objectivity of television news reporting of the 1972 presidential campaign. *Central States Speech Journal*, 24, 254–263.

Domke, D., Fan, D. P., Fibison, M., Shah, D. V., Smith, S. S., & Watts, M. D. (1997). News media, candidates and issues, and public opinion in the 1996 presidential campaign. *Journalism and Mass Communication Quarterly*, 74, 718–737.

Einsiedel, E. F., & Bibbee, M. J. (1979). The news magazines and minority candidates–campaign '76. *Journalism Quarterly*, 56, 102–105.

Evarts, D., & Stempel, G. H. (1974). Coverage of the 1972 campaign by TV, news magazines and major newspapers. *Journalism Quarterly*, 51, 645–648.

Fan, D. P. (1996). Predictions of the Bush-Clinton-Perot presidential race from the press. *Political Analysis*, 6, 67–105.

Farnsworth, S. J., & Lichter, S. R. (2011). Network television's coverage of the 2008 presidential election. *American Behavioral Scientist*, 55, 354–370.

Fico, F., & Cote, W. (1999). Fairness and balance in the structural characteristics of newspaper stories on the 1996 presidential election. *Journalism and Mass Communication Quarterly*, 76, 124–137.

Fico, F., Zeldes, G. A., Carpenter, S. & Diddi, A. (2008). Broadcast and cable network news coverage of the 2004 presidential election: An assessment of partisan and structural imbalance. *Mass Communication and Society*, 11, 319–339.

Fisher, J. (2001). Liberal bias in the South Bend Tribune. [Online.] Downloaded 1/18/06 from http://www.iusb.edu/~journal/2001/Fisher.html

Frank, R. S. (1973). *Message Dimensions of Television News*. Lexington, MA: Lexington Books.

Friedman, H. S., Mertz, T. I., & DiMatteo, M. R. (1980). Perceived bias in the facial expressions of television news broadcasters. *Journal of Communication*, 30, 103–111.

Graber, D. A. (1971). Press coverage patterns of campaign news: The 1968 presidential race. *Journalism Quarterly*, 48, 502–512.

Graber, D. A. (1976). Effect of incumbency on coverage patterns in 1972 presidential campaign. *Journalism Quarterly*, 53, 499–508.

Hayes, D. (2008). Party reputations, journalistic expectations: How issue ownership influences election news. *Political Communication*, 25, 377–400.

Hayes, D. (2010). The dynamics of agenda convergence and the paradox of competitiveness in presidential campaigns. *Political Research Quarterly*, 63, 594–611.

Higbie, C. E. (1954). Wisconsin dailies in the 1952: Space and display. *Journalism Quarterly*, 31, 56–60.

Hofstetter, C. R. (1978). News bias in the 1972 campaign: A cross-media comparison. *Journalism Monographs*, 58, 1–30.

Hofstetter, C. R., & Zukin, C. (1979). TV network news and advertising in the Nixon and McGovern campaigns. *Journalism Quarterly*, 56, 106–115, 152.

Hooker, J., Beedon, J., Bill, T., & Pallamy, C. (2001). Campaign coverage in *Time, Newsweek* and *US News and World Report*: An analysis of media bias. Paper presented to the National Communication Association, Atlanta.

Jamieson, K. H. (2000). *Everything You Think You Know About Politics...and Why You're Wrong*. New York: New Republic Books.

Joslyn, M.R, & Seccoli, S. (1996). Attentiveness to television news and opinion change in the fall 1996 presidential campaign. *Political Behavior*, 18, 141–170.

Just, M. R. (1997). Candidate strategies and the media campaign. In Pomper, G. (ed.). *The Election of 1996*. Chatham, NJ: Chatham House.

Kenney, K., & Simpson, C. (1993). Was coverage of the 1988 presidential race by Washington's two major dailies biased? *Journalism Quarterly*, 70, 345–355.

Kim, S. (2009). Different perspectives, different coverage: An exploratory analysis of news coverage of presidential candidates in 2008 presidential elections. [Online.] Downloaded 12 August 2011 from http://cim.anadolu.edu.tr/pdf/2009/1.Soohee. pdf

King, E. G. (1995). The flawed characters in the campaign: Prestige newspaper assessments of the 1992 presidential candidates' integrity and competence. *Journalism and Mass Communication Quarterly*, 72, 84–87.

Klein, M. W., & Maccoby, N. (1954). Newspaper objectivity in the 1952 campaign. *Journalism Quarterly*, 31, 285–296.

Kobre, S. (1953). How Florida dailies handles the 1952 presidential campaign. *Journalism Quarterly*, 30, 163–169.

Lee, C. (2002). Content analysis of the 2000 presidential election. *Southwestern Mass Communication Journal*, 17, 62–72.

Lee, D. E. (2010). Assessing media bias in the 2008 presidential election. Unpublished Bachelor's thesis, James Madison University.

Lee, T., Ryan, W. E., Wanta, W., Chang, K. (2004). Looking presidential: A comparison of newspaper photographs of candidates in the United States and Taiwan. *Asian Journal of Communication*, 14, 121–139.

Lichter, S. R. (2001). A plague on both parties: Substance and fairness in TV election news. *Press/Politics*, 6, 8-30.

Lowry, D. T. (1974). Measures of network news bias in the 1972 presidential campaign. *Journal of Broadcasting*, 18, 387–402.

Lowry, D. T., & Shidler, J. A. (1995). The sound bites, the biters and the bitten: An analysis of network TV news bias in campaign '92. *Journalism and Mass Communication Quarterly*, 72, 33–44.

Lowry, D. T., & Shidler, J. A. (1998). The sound bites, the biters, and the bitten: A two-campaign test of the anti-incumbency bias hypothesis in network TV news. *Journalism and Mass Communication Quarterly*. 75, 719–729.

Lowry, D. T. and Xie, L. (2007). Agenda-setting and framing by topic proximity: A new technique for the computerized content analysis of network TV news presidential campaign coverage. Paper presented to the annual convention of the International Communication Association, San Francisco.

Malaney, G. D., & Buss, T. F. (1979). AP wire reports vs. CBS TV news coverage of a presidential campaign. *Journalism Quarterly*, 56, 602–610.

Mantler, G., & Whiteman, D. (1995). Attention to candidates and issues in newspaper coverage of 1992 presidential campaign. *Newspaper Research Journal*, 16, 14–28.

McCluskey, M. E. (2005). A content analysis of 2004 presidential election headlines of the *Los Angeles Times* and the *Washington Times*. Unpublished master's thesis, University of Central Florida.

McCord, L. L., & Weaver, J. B. (1996). Biased coverage of the 1992 US presidential campaign in *Time, Newsweek*, and *US News and World Report*. Paper presented to the Speech Communication Association convention, San Diego, CA.

Meadow, R. G. (1973). Cross-media comparison of coverage of the 1972 presidential campaign. *Journalism Quarterly*, 50, 482–488.

Miller, A. B. (2005). Question of bias: A content analysis of the visual coverage of the 2004 presidential campaign. Unpublished master's thesis, Brigham Young University.

Millspaugh, M. (1949). Baltimore newspapers and the presidential election. *Public Opinion Quarterly*, 13, 122–123.

Moriarty, S. E., & Garramone, G. M. (1987). A study of newsmagazine photographs of the 1984 presidential campaign. *Journalism Quarterly*, 64, 728–734.

Moriarty, S. E, and Popovich, M. N. (1991). Newsmagazines visuals and the 1988 presidential election. *Journalism Quarterly*, 68, 371–380.

Mullen, B., Futrell, D., Stairs, D., Tice, D. M., Baumeister, R. F., Dawson, K. E., Riordan, C. A., Radloff, C. E., Goethals, G. E., Kennedy, J. G., & Rosenfeld, P. (1986). Newscasters' facial expressions and voting behavior of viewers: Can a smile elect a president? *Journal of Personality and Social Psychology*, 51, 291–295.

Murphy, J. (1998). An analysis of political bias in evening network news during the 1996 presidential campaigns. Unpublished doctoral dissertation, University of Oklahoma.

Nollet, M. A. (1968). The *Boston Globe* in four presidential elections. *Journalism Quarterly*, 45, 531–532.

Patterson, T. E. (1989). The press and its missed assignment. In Nelson, M. (ed.). *The Election of 1988*. Washington, DC: Congressional Quarterly Press.

Popovich, M., Moriarty, S., & Pitts, B. (1993). News magazine coverage of the 1988 presidential campaign. *Mass Communication Review*, 20, 99–111.

Price, G. (1954). A method for analyzing newspaper campaign coverage. *Journalism Quarterly*, 31, 447–458.

Pritchard, D. (2002). Viewpoint diversity in cross-owned newspapers and television stations: A study of news coverage of the 2000 presidential campaign. Federal Communications Commission Media Ownership Working Group paper. [Online.] Downloaded from http://hraunfoss.fcc.gov/edocs_public/attachmatch/DOC-226838A7.doc

Project for Excellence in Journalism (2000). The last lap: How the press covered the final stages of the Presidential campaign. [Online.] Downloaded 7/22/2010 from http://www.journalism.org/node/309

Project for Excellence in Journalism (2008). The color of news: How different media have covered the general election. [Online.] Downloaded 8/12/2011 from http://www.journalism.org/sites/journalism.org/files/The_COLOR_OF_NEWS_FINAL.pdf

Repass, D. E., & Chaffee, S. H. (1968). Administration vs. campaign coverage of two presidents in eight partisan dailies. *Journalism Quarterly*, 45, 528–531.

Robinson, M. J. (1983). Just how liberal is the news? 1980 revisited. *Public Opinion*, 7, 55–60.

Robinson, M. J. (1985). The media in campaign 1984: Part II wingless, toothless, and hopeless. *Public Opinion*, 9, 43–48.

Robinson, M. J., & Sheehan, M. A. (1983). *Over the Wire and on TV*. New York: Russell Sage Foundation.

Semetko, H. A., Blumler, J. G., Gurevich, M. & Weaver, D. H. (1991). *The Formation of Campaign Agendas: A Comparative Analysis of Party and Media Roles in Recent American and British Elections*. Hillsdale, NJ: Lawrence Erlbaum Associates.

Shaw, D. R. (1999). The impact of news media favorability and candidate events in presidential campaigns. *Political Communication*, 16, 183–202.

Shaw, D. R., & Sparrow, B. H. (1999). From the inner ring out: News convergence, cue-taking, and campaign coverage. *Political Research Quarterly*, 52, 323–351.

Staten, C. L., and Sloss, G .S. (1993). The media and politics: A content analysis of the *Louisville Courier-Journal* during the 1992 presidential election. *Journal of Political Science*, 21, 90–98.

Stempel, G. H. (1961). The prestige press covers the 1960 presidential campaign. *Journalism Quarterly*, 38, 157–163.

Stempel, G. H. (1965). The prestige press in two presidential elections. *Journalism Quarterly*, 42, 15–21.

Stempel, G. H. (1969). The prestige press meets the third-party challenge. *Journalism Quarterly*, 46, 699–706.

Stempel, G. H. (1991). How the news magazines covered the 1984 and 1988 campaigns. In Stempel, G. H., & Windhauser, J. W. (eds.). *The Media in the 1984 and 1988 Presidential Campaigns*. New York: Greenwood.

Stempel, G. H., & Windhauser, J. W. (1984). The prestige press revisited: coverage of the 1980 presidential campaign. *Journalism Quarterly*, 61, 49–55.

Stempel, G. H., & Windhauser, J. W. (1989). Coverage by the prestige press of the 1988 presidential campaign. *Journalism Quarterly*, 66, 894–896, 919.

Stempel, G. H. & Windhauser, J. W. (1991). Newspaper coverage of the 1984 and 1988 campaigns. In Stempel, G. H., & Windhauser, J. W. (eds.). *The Media in the 1984 and 1988 Presidential Campaigns*. New York: Greenwood.

Stevenson, R. L., Eisinger, R. A., Feinberg, B. M., & Kotok, A. B. (1973). Untwisting *The News Twisters*: A replication of Efron's study. *Journalism Quarterly*, 50, 211–219.

Stovall, J. G. (1985). The third-party challenge of 1980: News coverage of the presidential candidates. *Journalism Quarterly*, 62, 266–271.

Stovall, J. G. (1988). Coverage of 1984 presidential campaign. *Journalism Quarterly*, 65, 443–449, 484.

Terry, C. (2005). Milwaukee's radio news trinity: Clear Channel, Journal Communications and Wisconsin Public Radio and coverage of the 2004 election. Unpublished Master's thesis, University of Wisconsin-Milwaukee.

Vavreck, L. (2003). High fidelity? Presidential campaign coverage and the lack of media accountability. Paper presented to the annual convention of the American Political Science Association, Philadelphia.

Waldman, P., & Devitt, J. (1998). Newspaper photographs and the 1996 presidential election: The question of bias. *Journalism and Mass Communication Quarterly*, 75, 302–311.

Wang, X. (2003). Media Ownership and Objectivity. Unpublished Master's thesis, Louisiana State University.

Windhauser, J. W. & Evarts, D. R. (1991). Watching the campaigns on network television. In Stempel, G. H., & Windhauser, J. W. (eds.). *The Media in the 1984 and 1988 Presidential Campaigns*. New York: Greenwood.

Woodard, J. D. (1994). Coverage of elections on evening television news shows: 1972-1992. In Miller, A. H., & Gronbeck, B. E. (eds.). *Presidential Campaigns and American Self Images*. Boulder, CO: Westview.

Zeldes, G. A., Fico, F., Carpenter, S., & Diddi, A. (2008). Partisan balance and bias in network coverage of the 2000 and 2004 presidential elections. *Journal of Broadcasting and Electronic Media*, 52, 563–580.

References

Agnew, S. (1969a). Television news coverage. *Vital Speeches of the Day*, 36(4), 98–101.

Agnew, S. (1969b). The newspaper monopoly. *Vital Speeches of the Day*, 36(4), 133–136.

Ahrens, F. (2007). Chicago magnate to control Tribune; media firm to go private in $13 billion deal. *Washington Post*, April 3, D–1.

Altschull, J. H. (1984). *Agents of Power: The Role of the News Media in Human Affairs*. New York: Longman.

Ambrose, S. E. (1987). *Nixon: The Education of a Politician 1913–1962*. New York: Simon and Shuster.

Answers.com (2010). What is the most liberal newspaper in the US? (Online.) Downloaded 10/9/2010 from http://wiki.answers.com/Q/What_is_the_most _liberal_newspaper_in_the_US

ASNE (2001). Examining our credibility: Building trust. A report of the American Society of Newspaper Editors Journalism Credibility Project.

Associate Press Financial Wire (2005). Sinclair Shareholder Lawsuit Dropped. Feb. 24.

Babad, E. (2005). The psychological price of media bias. *Journal of Experimental Psychology: Applied*, 11(4), 245–255.

Babbie, E. (2001). *The Practice of Social Research* (9th Ed.). Belmont, CA: Wadsworth.

Bagdikian, B. H. (1971). *The Information Machines*. New York: Harper and Row.

Bagdikian, B. H. (1972). The politics of American newspapers. *Columbia Journalism Review*, March/April, 8–13.

Baron, D. P. (2006) Persistent media bias. *Journal of Public Economics*, 90, 1–36.

Barranco, D. A., & Shyles, L. (1988). Arab vs. Israeli news coverage in the *New York Times*, 1976 and 1984. *Journalism Quarterly*, 65(2), 178–181, 225.

Barrett, A. W., & Barrington, L. W. (2005). Bias in newspaper photograph selection. *Political Research Quarterly*, 58(4), 609–618.

Batlin, R. (1954). San Francisco newspapers' campaign coverage: 1896, 1952. *Journalism Quarterly*, 31, 297–303.

Benoit, W. L., Stein, K. A., & Hansen, G. J. (2005). *New York Times* coverage of presidential campaigns. *Journalism and Mass Communication Quarterly*, 82, 356–376.

Berelson, B. R., Lazarsfeld, P. F., & McPhee, W. N. (1954). *Voting: A Study of Opinion Formation in a Presidential Campaign*. Chicago: University of Chicago Press.

Blumberg, N. B. (1954). *One Party Press? Coverage of the 1952 Presidential Campaign in 35 Daily Newspapers*. Lincoln: University of Nebraska Press.

Bozell, L. B., & Baker, B. H. (1990). *And That's the Way It Isn't: A Reference Guide to Media Bias*. Alexandria, VA: Media Research Center.

Breed, W. (1955). Social control in the newsroom: A functional analysis. *Social Forces*, 33, 326–335.

Brown, R. U. (1960). 57% of U.S. dailies back Nixon; 16% for Kennedy. *Editor & Publisher*, November 5, 9–13.

Buffett, W. (2009). Transcript from interview from May 4, 2009, on CNBC. (Online.) Downloaded 10/7/2010 from http://www.lioninvestor.com/code/uploads/warren
–buffett–may09–transcript.pdf.

Bumiller, E. (2008). How internal battles divided the McCain and Palin camps. *The New York Times*, November 6, P9.

Busterna, J. C., & Hansen, K. A. (1990). Presidential endorsement patterns by chain–owned papers, 1976–1984. *Journalism Quarterly*, 67(2), 286–294.

Carter, S., Fico, F., & McCabe, J. A. (2002). Partisan and structural balance in local television election coverage. *Journalism and Mass Communication Quarterly*, 79, 41–53.

Center for Media and Public Affairs (CMPA). (2004). Campaign 2004 final: How TV news covered the general election campaign. *Media Monitor*, XVIII(6).

Center for Media and Public Affairs (CMPA). (2009). Election watch: Campaign 2008 final: How TV news covered the general election campaign. *Media Monitor*, XXIII(1).

Chancellor, J., & Mears, W. R. (1995). *The New News Business: A Guide to Writing and Reporting*. New York: Harper Collins.

Chinlund, C. (2004). Endorsements: Who decides for the Globe? *Boston Globe*, October 25, A15.

Clancey, M., & Robinson, M. J. (1985). The media in campaign '84: General election coverage Part I. *Public Opinion*, 8, 49–54, 59.

Compaine, B. (1980). *The Newspaper Industry in the 1980's: An Assessment of Economics and Technology*. White Plains, N.Y.: Knowledge Industry Publications.

Cook, T. D., & Campbell, D. T. (1979). *Quasiexperimentation: Design and Analysis Issues for Field Settings*. Chicago: Rand McNally.

Cooper, M., & Soley, L. C. (1990). All the right sources. *Mother Jones*, 15(2), 20–27, 45–46.

Crouse, T. (1973). *The Boys on the Bus*. New York: Random House.

Culbertson, H. M., & Stempel, G. H. (1991). Public attitudes about coverage and awareness of editorial endorsements. In Stempel, G. H., & Windhauser, J. W. (eds.). *The Media in the 1984 and 1988 Presidential Campaigns.* New York: Greenwood Press.

D'Alessio, D., (2003). An experimental examination of readers' perceptions of media bias. *Journalism and Mass Communication Quarterly*, 80, 282–294.

D'Alessio, D., & Allen, M. (2000). Media bias in presidential elections: A meta–analysis. *Journal of Communication*, 50, 133–156.

D'Alessio, D., & Allen, M. (2002). Selective exposure and dissonance after decisions. *Psychological Reports*, 91, 527–532.

D'Alessio, D., & Allen, M. (2006). On the role of newspaper ownership in presidential campaign coverage by newspapers. In Priess, R. W., Gayle, B. M., Burrell, N., Allen, M., & Bryant, J. (eds.). *Mass Media Effects Research: Advances through Meta–Analysis.* Mahwah, NJ: Lawrence Erlbaum Associates.

Dalton, R. M., Beck, P. A., & Huckfeldt, R. (1998). Partisan cues and the media: Information flows in the 1992 presidential election. *American Political Science Review*, 92, 111–126.

Danielson, W. A., & Adams, J. B. (1961). Completeness of press coverage of the 1960 campaign. *Journalism Quarterly*, 38, 441–452.

Dautrich, K., & Hartley, T. H. (1999). *How the News Media Fail American Voters.* New York: Columbia University Press.

Davis, J. (1982). Sexist bias in eight newspapers. *Journalism Quarterly*, 59(4), 456–460.

DellaVigna, S., & Kaplan, E. (2007). The Fox News effect: Media bias and voting. *The Quarterly Journal of Economics*, 122(3), 1187–1234.

Doll, H. D., & Bradley, B. E. (1974). A study of the objectivity of television news reporting of the 1972 presidential campaign. *Central States Speech Journal*, 24, 254–263.

Donohew, L. (1967). Newspaper gatekeepers and forces in the news channel. *The Public Opinion Quarterly*, 31, 61–68.

Druckman, J. N., & Parkin, M. (2005). The impact of media bias: How editorial slant affects voters. *The Journal of Politics*, 67, 1030–1049.

Editor & Publisher (1958). Nation's Editors Pick 15 'Superior' Papers. April 2, 12.

Editor & Publisher (1996). Newspaper endorsements for President since 1940. October 26, 13.

Efron, E., (1971). *The News Twisters.* Los Angeles: Nash Publishing.

Epstein, E. J. (1973). *News from Nowhere: Television and the News.* New York: Random House.

Evarts, D., & Stempel, G. H. (1974). Coverage of the 1972 campaign by TV, news magazines and major newspapers. *Journalism Quarterly*, 51, 645–648.

Farnsworth, S. J., & Lichter, S. R. (2007). *The Nightly News Nightmare: Television's Coverage of U.S. Presidential Elections, 1988–2004* (2nd ed.). Lanham, MD: Rowan and Littlefield.

Festinger, L. (1957). *A Theory of Cognitive Dissonance.* Stanford, CA: Stanford University Press.

Fico, F., & Cote, W. (1999). Fairness and balance in the structural characteristics of newspaper stories on the 1996 presidential election. *Journalism and Mass Communication Quarterly*, 76, 124–137.

Fico, F., Zeldes, G. A., Carpenter, S. & Diddi, A. (2008). Broadcast and cable network news coverage of the 2004 presidential election: An assessment of partisan and structural imbalance. *Mass Communication and Society*, 11, 319–339.

Fisher, J. (2001). Liberal bias in the South Bend Tribune. [Online.] Downloaded 1/18/06 from http://www.iusb.edu/~journal/2001/Fisher.html

Fitzgerald, V. M. (1995). Public opinion polls and network news coverage of presidential campaigns. Paper presented to the annual convention of the Speech Communications Association, San Antonio.

Foot, K. A., & Schneider, S. M. (2002). Online action in campaign 2000: An exploratory analysis of the US political web sphere. *Journal of Broadcasting and Electronic Media*, 46, 222–244.

Frank, R. S. (1973). *Message Dimensions of Television News.* Lexington, MA: Lexington Books.

Gans, H. J. (1979). *Deciding What's News.* New York: Pantheon.

Garbeau, G. (1992). Clinton's the choice. Editor & Publisher, October 24, 9–11, 44–45.

Gartner, D., & Gartner, T. (1998). *You Have More Than You Think.* New York: Simon & Shuster.

Gelb, A. (2003). *City Room.* New York: Berkeley Books.

Giner–Sorolla, R., & Chaiken, S. (1994). The causes of hostile media judgments. *Journal of Experimental Social Psychology*, 30, 165–180.

Giobbe, D. (1996). Dole wins . . . in endorsements. *Editor & Publisher*, October 26, 7–11.

Goldberg, B. (2003). *Bias: A CBS Insider Exposes How the Media Distort the News.* Washington, D.C.: Regnery.

Gosselin, K. R. (2011). *Courant* trims newsroom jobs. *Hartford Courant*, July 7, 2011.

Graber, D. A. (1971). Press coverage patterns of campaign news: The 1968 presidential race. *Journalism Quarterly*, 48, 502–512.

Graber, D. A. (1976). Effects of incumbency on coverage patterns in 1972 presidential campaign. *Journalism Quarterly*, 53(4), 499–508.

Graber, D. A. (1997). *Mass Media and American Politics.* Washington, DC: Congressional Quarterly Press.

Groseclose, T., & Milyo, J. (2005). A measure of media bias. *The Quarterly Journal of Economics*, 120, 1191–1237.

Gunter, B. (1997). *Measuring Bias on Television.* Luton, UK: University of Luton Press.

Gunther, A. C., & Christen, C. T. (2002). Projection or persuasive press? Contrary effects of personal opinion and perceived news coverage on estimates of public opinion. *Journal of Communication*, 52, 177–195.

Gunther, A. C., & Schmitt, K. (2004). Mapping boundaries of the hostile media effect. *Journal of Communication*, 54(1), 55–70.

Halberstam, D. (1979). The Powers That Be. New York: A. A. Knopf.

Hallin, D. C. (1992). Sound bite news: Television coverage of elections, 1968–1988. *Journal of Communication*, 42, 5–24.

Hastorf, A. H., & Cantril, H. (1954). They saw a game: A case study. *Journal of Abnormal and Social Psychology*, 49, 129–134.

Hauser, G. A. (1999). *Vernacular Voices: The Rhetoric of Publics and Public Spheres*. Columbia, SC: University of South Carolina Press.

Hayes, A. A., & Murray, S. G. (1998). Why do the news media cover certain candidates more than others? The antecedents of state and national news coverage in the 1992 presidential nomination campaign. *American Politics Research*, 26, 420–438.

Heinlein, R. A. (1992). *Take Back Your Government!* New York: Baen.

Hill, G. (1962). Nixon denounces press as biased. The New York Times, Nov 8, 1, 18.

History Channel (2008). Richard M. Nixon concedes defeat in gubernatorial election. [Audio] Accessed 6/17/08 at http://www.history.com/media.do?id=v4t5&action.clip

Hoffman, A. J., & Wallach, J. (2007). The effects of media bias. *Journal of Applied Social Psychology*, 37(3), 616–630.

Hofstetter, C. R. (1978). News bias in the 1972 campaign: a cross-media comparison. *Journalism Monographs*, 58, 1-30.

Hunter, J. E., & Schmidt, F. L. (1990). *Methods of Meta–Analysis: Correcting Error and Bias in Research Findings*. Newbury Park: Sage.

Hunter, J. E., Schmidt, F. L., & Jackson, G. B. (1982). *Meta–Analysis: Cumulating Research Findings Across Studies*. Beverly Hills: Sage.

Jamieson, K. H. (2000). *Everything You Think You Know about Politics . . . And Why You're Wrong*. New York: New Republic Books.

Jamieson, K. H. (2006). *Electing the President 2004: The Insiders' View*. Philadelphia: University of Pennsylvania Press.

Jefferson, T. (1787/2006). Letter to Edward Carrington. Downloaded 12/20 from http://etext.virginia.edu/jefferson/quotations/jeff1600.htm

Johnson, G. W. (1926). *What Is News? A Tentative Outline*. New York: Alfred A. Knopf.

Journal Communications, (2007). 2007 Annual Report. Milwaukee, WI: Journal Communications.

Kahn, K. F., & Kenney, P. J. (2002). The slant of the news: How editorial endorsements influence campaign coverage and citizens' views of candidates. *American Political Science Review*, 96, 381–394.

Kang, J. S. (2007). Economics of newspapers' presidential endorsement decisions: Evidence of endogenous product–type choices of media firms. Paper presented to International Communication Association, San Francisco.

Katz, E., & Lazarsfeld, P. F. (1955). *Personal Influence: The Part Played by People in the Flow of Mass Communication*. Glencoe, IL: Free Press.

Kenney, K., & Simpson, C. (1993). Was coverage of the 1988 presidential race by Washington's major dailies biased? *Journalism Quarterly*, 70, 345–355.

Kern, M. (2001). Disadvantage Al Gore in election 2000: Coverage of issue and candidate attributes, including candidate as campaigner, on newspaper and television news web sites. *American Behavioral Scientist*, 44, 2125–2139.

King, E. G. (1995). The flawed characters in the campaign: prestige newspaper assessments of the 1992 Presidential candidates' integrity and competence. *Journalism and Mass Communication Quarterly*, 72, 84-87.

Kinney, J. (1988). *Walt Disney and Other Assorted Characters*. New York: Harmony Books.

Klapper, J. (1961). *The Effects of Mass Communication*. Glencoe, IL: Free Press.

Klein, M. W., & Maccoby, N. (1954). Newspaper objectivity in the 1952 campaign. *Journalism Quarterly*, 31, 285–296.

Kobre, S. (1953). How Florida dailies handled the 1952 presidential campaign. *Journalism Quarterly*, 30, 163–169.

Krippendorf, K. (2003). *Content Analysis: An Introduction to its Methodology* (2nd ed.). Thousand Oaks, CA: Sage.

Lee, T. T., Ryan, W. R., Wanta, W., & Chang, K. K. (2004). Looking presidential: A comparison of newspaper photographs of candidates in the United States and Taiwan. *Asian Journal of Communication*, 14, 121–139.

Lefever, E. W. (1974). *TV and National Defense: An Analysis of CBS News, 1972–1973*. Boston, VA: Institute for American Strategy.

Levine, T. R. & Asada, K. J. K. (2007). Sample sizes and effect sizes are negatively correlated in meta–analyses: Evidence and implications of a publication bias against non–significant findings. Paper presented to the annual convention of the International Communications Association, San Francisco.

Leviticus (16:21). *The Holy Bible*. Authorized King James Version.

Lieberman, B. (2000). '*Tribune–Review*' covers half a campaign. *Editor & Publisher*, Nov. 13, 9–10.

Lieberman, T. (2000). *Slanting the Story: The Forces that Shape the News*. New York: The New Press.

Liebling, A. J. (1961/1975). *The Press*. New York: Pantheon.

Lin, N. (1976). *Foundations of Social Research*. New York: McGraw–Hill.

Lippmann, W. (1922/1991). *Public Opinion*. New Brunswick, NJ: Transaction.

Littlewood, T. B. (1999). *Calling Elections: The History of Horse-Race Journalism*. South Bend, IN: University of Notre Dame Press.

Lowry, D. T., & Shidler, J. A. (1998). The sound bites, the biters and the bitten: A two–campaign test of the anti–incumbent bias hypothesis in network TV news. *Journalism and Mass Communication Quarterly*, 75, 719–729.

Lowry, D. T. & Xie, L. (2007). Agenda–setting and framing by topic proximity: Anew technique for the computerized content analysis of network TV news presidential campaign coverage. Paper presented to the annual convention of the International Communication Association, San Francisco.

Malaney, G. D., & Buss, T. F. (1979). AP wire reports vs. CBS TV news coverage of a Presidential campaign. *Journalism Quarterly*, 56, 602-610.

Mankiewicz, F. (1989). From Lippmann to Letterman: The 10 most powerful voices. *Gannett Center Journal*, 3(2).

Markham, J. W. (1961). Press treatment of the 1958 state elections in Pennsylvania. *Political Research Quarterly*, 14, 912–924.

Martindale, C. (1985). Coverage of black Americans in five newspapers since 1950. *Journalism Quarterly*, 62, 321–328, 436.

Mayeaux, P. E. (1996). *Broadcast News: Writing and Reporting* (2nd ed.). Madison, WI: Brown and Benchmark.

McGinnis, J. (1969). *The Selling of the President, 1968.* New York: Pocket Books.

McQuail, D. (1987). *Mass Communication Theory: An Introduction* (2nd ed.). London: Sage.

Meiklejohn, A. (1948). *Free Speech and Its Relation to Self–Government.* New York: Harper.

Miller, G. R., & Nicholson, H. E. (1976). *Communication Inquiry: A Perspective on a Process.* Reading, MA: Addison–Wesley.

Millspaugh, M. (1949). Baltimore newspapers and the presidential election. *Public Opinion Quarterly*, 13, 122–123.

Mitchell, G. (2000). Bird in the hand for Bush? *Editor & Publisher*, Nov. 6, 24–27.

Moriarty, S. E., & Garramone, G. M. (1987). A study of newsmagazine photographs of the 1984 Presidential campaign. *Journalism Quarterly*, 64, 728–734.

Musgrave, A. (1974). Logical versus historical theories of confirmation. *The British Journal for the Philosophy of Science*, 25, 1–23.

Neiva, E. M. (1996). Chain building: The consolidation of the American newspaper industry, 1953–1980. *The Business History Review*, 70, 1–42.

New York Times (1952). Mr. Stevenson and the press. Sept. 9, 30.

New York Times (1962). Transcript of Nixon's news conference on his defeat by Brown in race for governor of California, Nov. 8, 18–19.

Niven, D. (2002). *Tilt? The Search for Media Bias.* Westport, CT: Praeger.

Niven, D., Lichter, S. R., & Amundson, D. (2003). The political content of late night comedy. *Press/Politics*, 8, 118–133.

Nixon, R. M. (1978). *The Memoirs of Richard Nixon.* New York: Grossett and Dunlap.

Norris, P., & Sanders, D. (1998). Does balance matter? Experiments in TV news. Paper presented to the American Political Science Association, Boston, Sept. 3–6.

Okrent, D. (2004) The public editor: Is *The New York Times* a liberal newspaper? The *New York Times*, July 25.

Ostroff, D. H., & Sandell, K. L. (1989). Campaign coverage by local TV news in Columbus, Ohio, 1978–1986. *Journalism Quarterly*, 66, 114–120.

Page, B. I., & Shapiro, R. Y. (1992). *The Rational Public: Fifty Years of Trends in Americans' Policy Preferences.* Chicago: University of Chicago Press.

Paraschos, M., & Rutherford, B. (1985). Newspaper news coverage of invasion of Lebanon by Israel in 1982. *Journalism Quarterly*, 62, 457–464.

Patterson, T. E. (1993). Out of Order. New York: Alfred A. Knopf.

Patterson, T. E. & Donsbach, W. (1996). New decisions: Journalists as partisan actors. *Political Communication*, 13, 455–468.

Petty, R. E., Ostrom, T. M., & Brock, T. C. (1981). *Cognitive Responses in Persuasion.* Hillsdale, NJ: Lawrence Erlbaum Associates.

Pournelle, J. E. (1992). Introduction. In Heinlein, R. A. *Take Back Your Government.* Riverdale, NY: Baen.

PR Newswire (2004). Stolen honor: Ex–DC bureau chief bares bias at Sinclair. Oct. 23.

Prior, M. (2006). The incumbent in the living room: The rise of television and the incumbency advantage in U.S. House elections. *The Journal of Politics*, 68, 657–673.

Pritchard, D. (2002). Viewpoint diversity in cross-owned newspapers and television stations: a study of news coverage of the 2000 Presidential campaign. Federal Communications Commission Media Ownership Working Group paper. [Online.] Downloaded from http://hraunfoss.fcc.gov/edocs_public/attachmatch/DOC-226838A7.doc

Project for Excellence in Journalism (2008). The color of news: How different media have covered the general election. [Online.] Downloaded 8/12/2011 from http://www.journalism.org/sites/journalism.org/files/The_COLOR_OF_NEWS_FINAL.pdf

Reuter, J., & Zitzewitz, E. (2006). Do ads influence editors? Advertising and bias in the financial media. *The Quarterly Journal of Economics*, 12, 197–227.

Rivers, W. L. (1965). *The Opinionmakers*. Boston: Beacon Press.

Rogers, E. M., Dearing, J. W., & Chang, S. (1991). AIDS in the 1980's: The agenda setting process for a public issue. *Journalism Monographs*, 126, entire.

Rosen, J. (2004). Resigning in protest: Two editors quit their Florida newspaper after it makes an election policy exception for one candidate. *American Journalism Review*, April 1.

Rosenthal, R. (1991). *Meta–Analytic Procedures for Social Research* (rev. ed.). Newbury Park: Sage.

Ross, I. (1968). *The Loneliest Campaign: The Truman Victory of 1948*. New York: Signet.

Rubin, D. (2004). Sinclair to air only part of Kerry film: Amid rising pressure it said portions of *Stolen Honor* would be included in a one–hour program. *Philadelphia Inquirer*, Oct. 20, A16.

Rucker, B. W. (1960). News services' crowd reporting in the 1956 presidential campaign. *Journalism Quarterly*, 37, 195–198.

Schieffer, B. (2003). *This Just In: What I Couldn't Tell You on TV*. New York: G. P. Putnam's Sons.

Schiffer, A. J. (2006). Assessing partisan bias in political news: The case of local senate election coverage. *Political Communication*, 23, 23–39.

Schmitt, K. M., Gunther, A. C., & Liebhart, J. L. (2004). Why partisans see mass media as biased. *Communication Research*, 31, 623–640.

Schulhofer–Wohl, S., & Garrido, M. (2009). Do newspapers matter? Short-run and long–run evidence from the closure of the Cincinnati Post. National Bureau of Economic Research Working Paper 14817. [Online.] Downloaded from http://www.nber.org/papers/w14817 on August 24, 2011.

Schulte, H. H., & DuFresne, M. P. (2004). *Getting the Story*. New York: Macmillan.

Schwartz, J. (2002). *Associated Press Reporting Handbook*. New York: McGraw–Hill.

Seelye, K. Q. (1996). Dole assails White House as 'Animal House' of 'elitists.' *The New York Times*, Oct. 28, A15.

Shoemaker, P. J., and Reese, S. D. (1996). *Mediating the Message: Theories of Influences on Mass Media Content* (2nd ed.). White Plains, NY: Longman.

Sigelman, L. (1973). Reporting the news: An organizational analysis. *The American Journal of Sociology*, 79, 132–155.

Silver, D. (1986). A comparison of newspaper coverage of male and female officials in Michigan. *Journalism Quarterly*, 63, 144–149.

Smith, K. B. (1997). When all's fair: Signs of parity in media coverage of female candidates. *Political Communication*, 14, 71–82.

Smith, T. J. (1990). Liberal and conservative trends in the United States since World War II. *Public Opinion Quarterly*, 54, 479–507.

St. Dizier, B. (1986). Republican endorsements, Democratic positions: An editorial page contradiction. *Journalism Quarterly*, 63, 581–586.

Stebenne, D. (1993). Media coverage of American presidential elections: A historical perspective. In Freedom Forum Media Studies Center, *The Media and Campaign '92: The Finishing Line: Covering the Campaign's Final Days*. New York: Freedom Forum Media Studies Center.

Stempel, G. H. (1961). The prestige press covers the 1960 presidential campaign. *Journalism Quarterly*, 38, 157–163.

Stempel, G. H. (2011). Personal communication to author.

Stempel, G. H., & Windhauser, J. W. (1989). Coverage by the prestige press of the 1988 Presidential campaign. *Journalism Quarterly*, 66, 894-896, 919.

Stevenson, R. L., Eisinger, R. A., Feinberg, B. M., & Kotok, A. B. (1973). Untwisting *The News Twisters*: A replication of Efron's study. *Journalism Quarterly*, 50, 211–219.

Stevenson, R. L., & Greene, M. T. (1980). A reconsideration of bias in the news. *Journalism Quarterly*, 57, 115–121.

Stovall, J. G. (1984). Incumbency and news coverage of the 1980 presidential election. *Western Political Quarterly*, 37, 621–631.

Straubhaar, J., & LaRose, R. (2006). *Media Now: Understanding Media, Culture and Technology* (5th ed.). Belmont, CA: Thomson–Wadsworth.

Sutter, D. (2001). Can the media be so liberal? The economics of media bias. *Cato Journal*, 20, 431–451.

Sutter, D. (2002). Advertising and political bias in the media: The market for criticism of the market economy. *American Journal of Economics*, 64(4), 725–745.

Terry, C. (2005). Milwaukee's radio news trinity: Clear Channel, Journal Communications and Wisconsin Public Radio and coverage of the 2004 election. Unpublished Master's thesis, University of Wisconsin-Milwaukee.

Thalheimer, M. (1993). Reflections and ruminations on campaign '92: The humorist's view. In Freedom Forum Media Studies Center, *The Media and Campaign '92: The Finishing Line: Covering the Campaign's Final Days*. New York: Freedom Forum Media Studies Center.

Thomas, H. (2006). *Watchdogs of Democracy? The Waning Washington Press Corps and How It Failed the Public*. New York: Scribner.

Thomas, L. (2007). Shareholders of Times Co. hold out 42% of board vote. *The New York Times*, April 25, C–6.

Thompson, H. S. (1973). *Fear and Loathing on the Campaign Trail '72*. New York: Popular Library.

Trimble, V. H. (ed.) (1948/1981). *Scripps–Howard Handbook*. Cincinnati, OH: The E. W. Scripps Company.

Truman, H. S (1952). The President's news conference of September 11th. (Online). Downloaded from http://www.presidency.ucsb.edu/ws/print.php?pid14247, on 8/29/2007.

United Press International (1982). Financial. May 17. BC Cycle.

Vallone, R. P., Ross, L., & Lepper, M. R. (1985). The hostile media phenomenon: Biased perceptions and perceptions of media bias in coverage of the Beirut massacre. *Journal of Personality and Social Psychology*, 49, 577–585.

Wagman, R. J. (1991). *The First Amendment Book*. New York. Pharos Books.

Wang, X. (2003). Media Ownership and Objectivity. Unpublished Master's thesis, Louisiana State University.

Washington Post (1984). Dailies make endorsements: Foreign, economic policies of candidates weighed. Oct. 29, A4.

Watts, M. D., Domke, D., Shah, D. V., & Fan, D. P. (1999). Elite cues and media bias in presidential campaigns. *Communication Research*, 26, 144–175.

Weaver, D. H., Beam, R. A., Brownlee, B. J., Vokes, P. S., & Wilhoit, G. C. (2007). *The American Journalist in the 21st Century: U.S. News People at the Dawn of a New Millenium. Mahwah*, NJ: Lawrence Erlbaum Associates.

Weaver, E., with Pluto, T. (1984). *Weaver on Strategy*. New York: Collier.

Welles, O. (Producer and Director), (1941). *Citizen Kane* [Film]. Available from The Nostalgia Merchant, Los Angeles.

Westerstahl, J. (1983). Objective news reporting. *Communication Research*, 10, 403–424.

Westley, B. H., Higbie, C. E., Burke, T., Lippert, D. J., Maurer, L., & Stone, V. A. (1963). The news magazines and the 1960 conventions. *Journalism Quarterly*, 40, 525–530, 647.

White, D. M. (1950). The gate–keeper: A case study in the selection of news. *Journalism Quarterly*, 27, 383–390.

Williams, A. (1975). Unbiased study of television news bias. *Journal of Communication*, 25, 190–199.

Wimmer, R. D., & Dominick, J. R. (2011). *Mass Media Research: An Introduction* (9th ed.). Boston, MA: Wadsworth.

Wortham, S., & Locher, M. (1996). Voicing on the news: An analytic technique for studying media bias. *Text: An Interdisciplinary Journal for the Study of Discourse*, 16, 557–585.

Xiang, Y., and Sarvary, M. (2007). News consumption and media bias. *Marketing Science*, 26, 611–628.

Yahoo.com (2010). What are the most liberal and conservative newspapers in the USA nowadays? [Online.] Downloaded 10/9/2010 from http://answers.yahoo.com/question/index?qid=2008062916

Zeldes, G. A., Fico, F., Carpenter, S., & Diddi, A. (2008). Partisan balance and bias in network coverage of the 2000 and 2004 presidential elections. *Journal of Broadcasting and Electronic Media*, 52, 563–580.

Index

new media outlets, as property, 30–34, 77; chain ownership, 33; models of, 32; public vs. private ownership, 32–34, 83–89

newspapers, 14, 28–29, 31–34, 56–57, 62–63, 68, 70–71, 75–83, 92–93, 103–105, 107, 109; as investments, 83; bias in, 31–32, 56–57, 70–71, 75–83, 92–93; endorsements by circulation, 107; historically black, 108

news values, 12, 19–21

The News Twisters, 46

The New York Times, 11, 26, 27, 32–33, 43, 54, 63, 68, 75, 85, 86, 94–96, 104, 111; "Arm of the DNC," 95, 113; bias in, 54, 94–96, 111; covering Nixon press conference, 11; ownership of, 32–33, 104

The New York Times Company, 88

Nixon, Richard, 1–3, 9, 16, 23, 36, 76, 91, 106, 108, 112–113, 115; addressing media, 1962, 1–3, 108, 110; media coverage of, 31, 76, 108–110

non-ideological biases, 23–24, 27–30, 38–39, 106; business–based, 27–30, 38–39; "Horse Race" journalism, 23–24; negative tone, 23–24, 106

number of studies across time, 64–65

Ochs/Sulzberger family, 25, 32, 39, 78, 104; Ochs, Adolph, 25

"One Party Press," 6, 64, 113; book entitled, 64; charges of, 6, 64

Origins of Ideological Bias, 77, 101; conservative viewpoint, 77, 101; liberal viewpoint, 77, 101

Otis/Chandler family, 30; Chandler, Otis 31

ownership of news media outlets, 19, 22, 30–34, 39, 83–89, 99, 101, 104–105; influence of on bias, 39,

83–89, 99, 101, 103–104; types of 104–105

Pittsburgh Tribune–Review, 31, 39, 81

presidential campaigns, 60–61; as a subject of study, 60–61

Prestige Press, 63, 79–80, 86, 87, 94, 107; as a moderator, 79–80, 86, 87; defined, 63

pro-incumbency bias, 93, 105–106; in newspapers, 93

public vs. private ownership of news media outlets, 83–89; biases in, 86–88; process of changing states, 88–89

publishers' preference for conservative ideology, 20, 38; measured, 20

Pulliam, Eugene, 31

reporters' preference for liberal ideology, 20, 38; measured, 20

Scaife, Richard Mellon, 31, 39, 81

scapegoating, 112

Schieffer, Bob, 25, 31

The Scripps-Howard Handbook, 12

Scripps-Howard newspapers, 56

The Selling of the President 1968, 1, 23

significance of findings, 69–72, 103; statistical, 69; sample vs. population, 71–72; substantive, 70–71

Sinclair Broadcasting, 33, 35; "Stolen Honor" incident, 33, 35

size of news hole, 11, 25–26; potential for bias in, 11, 26

Society of Professional Journalists, 56

Spanish language media, 108

Stevenson, Adlai, 16

subjectivity in reporting, 11–13

Time magazine, 31, 64, 72, 79, 85, 87; bias in reporting on "rubber-type army," 31

Tribune Company, 32